CANDLELIGHT SPELLS

Books by
Gerina Dunwich

Candlelight Spells

The Concise Lexicon of the Occult

Everyday Wicca

The Magick of Candle Burning

Magick Potions

The Modern Witch's Complete Sourcebook

Phantom Felines and Other Ghostly Animals

The Secrets of Love Magick

Wicca A to Z

The Wicca Book of Days

Wicca Candle Magick

The Wicca Garden

Wicca Love Spells

The Wicca Spellbook

The Wiccan's Dictionary of Prophecy and Omens

Your Magickal Cat

Available from Citadel Press/Kensington Publishing Corp.

CANDLELIGHT SPELLS

SPELLS

The Modern Witch's Book of Spellcasting, Feasting, and Natural Healing

GERINA DUNWICH

CITADEL PRESS
Kensington Publishing Corp.
www.kensingtonbooks.com

CITADEL PRESS BOOKS are published by

Kensington Publishing Corp.
119 West 40th Street
New York, NY 10018

All Kensington titles, imprints, and distributed lines are available at special quantity discounts for bulk purchases for sales promotions, premiums, fund-raising, educational, or institutional use.

Special book excerpts or customized printings can also be created to fit specific needs. For details, write or phone the office of the Kensington sales manager: Kensington Publishing Corp., 119 West 40th Street, New York, NY 10018, attn: Sales Department; phone 1-800-221-2647.

CITADEL PRESS and the Citadel logo are Reg. U.S. Pat. & TM Off.

ISBN: 978-0-8065-4125-9

First Citadel printing (revised edition): September 2021

20 19 18 17 16 15 14 13 12 11

Printed in the United States of America

Electronic edition:

ISBN: 978-0-8065-3950-8 (e-book)

To my Gemini love, AL JACKTER,
for always being there when I needed a friend.

*And with loving gratitude
to my stubborn Taurus mother
for all of her love, encouragement
and spiritual support.*

Contents

CANDLELIGHT
SPELLS

Introduction:
The Old Religion

WITCHCRAFT IS THE OLD RELIGION. It is often called the Craft of the Wise; a prospering nature-oriented religion that explores the hidden powers in woman and man. The magickal arts, herbalism, divination, the worship of both male and female deities, and celebration of the seasonal transitions are all part of the Old Religion, and despite a frightening and gruesome history of persecution, bloodshed, and misunderstanding, it has survived for thousands of years.

Witchcraft in England was made an illegal offense in the year 1541, and in 1604, a law decreeing capital punishment for witches was adopted. Forty years later, the thirteen colonies in America also made death the penalty for the "crime" of witchcraft. By the late 17th century, the loyal followers of the Old Religion were in hiding and witchcraft had turned into a secret underground religion after an estimated one million persons had been put to death in Europe and more than thirty condemned at Salem, Massachusetts, in the name of Christianity.

Although the infamous Salem witchcraft trials of 1692 are the most memorable and best-documented ones in the history of America, the first hanging of a witch in New England actually took place in Connecticut in 1647, forty-five years before the Salem witch hysteria. Other pre-Salem executions occurred in Providence, Rhode Island, in 1662.

The most popular method of witch extermination in New England was the gallows. In Europe, it was burning. Other methods included pressing to death, drowning, and fatal torture.

For 260 years following the last witch execution, the followers of the Old Religion kept their practices hidden behind the shadows of secrecy, and not until after the laws against witchcraft in England were finally repealed in 1951 did witches officially come out of the proverbial broom closet.

Witches today seek to live in harmony with nature and practice their ancient rites to attune themselves with the natural rhythms of life forces marked by the lunar cycle and the seasons. Witches do not accept the concept of innate sin or absolute evil, and they do not worship the Devil as defined by the Christian tradition.

Unfortunately, many people who are not familiar with the actual practices and philosophy of witchcraft are led to believe that witches are Devil-worshippers. This is a terrible misconception that stems from centuries of church propaganda, fear, and ignorance of the unknown. The fact of the matter is that witches do not believe in, receive their powers from, sign pacts with, or sell their souls to the Devil, as many people wrongly assume.

Also known as Satan, Lucifer, Beelzebub, and by many other names, the Devil is an entity in the Abrahamic religions, usually seen as a fallen angel, the personification of evil, and the adversary of God. Witchcraft, on the other hand, is a pre-Christian practice existing long before the advent of the Church or its concepts of Satan and Hell. The Devil played no role whatsoever in the Old Religion.

There are two main deities honored and worshipped in the rites of many modern witches: the Mother Goddess of Fertility and the Horned God. Their names vary from one witchcraft tradition to the next. Some traditions, such as the Gardnerians, use different deity names in both their higher and lower degrees.

The Goddess is the female principle and represents fertility and rebirth.

The moon is her symbol, and she is often depicted as having three faces, each representing a different lunar phase. She is the Virgin (or the Warrior Maid), the Mother, and the Wise Crone—the new moon, the full moon, and the waning moon.

The Goddess possesses many different names. She is often called Diana, Cerridwen, Freya, Isis, Ishtar, Kali, the Lady or any other name that a witch feels responds to her or his own mythopoeic vision.

In a coven, the Goddess is represented by the High Priestess and is usually worshipped in the spring and summer months, as she symbolizes the fertility of the earth in the growing time. Some feminist Dianic covens worship the Goddess as their sole deity, but most worship both the Horned God and the Goddess.

The Horned God, represented as a hirsute bearded man having the hooves and horns of a goat, is a god of nature and the male counterpart to the image of the Goddess. In primitive times, he was worshipped as the Horned God of Hunting, but has since become known as the "horned god of death and all that comes after."

Like the Goddess, the Horned God is also known by many different names. In some traditions of Wicca (a relatively modern pagan religion) he is called Cerunnos, which is Latin for "the Horned One." In others, he is known as Pan or Woden. The autumn and winter months are when the Horned God is usually worshipped, as he symbolizes the dark half of the year.

The worship of the Mother Goddess of Fertility and the Horned God symbolizes the witch's belief that everything existing in the universe is divided into female and male, negative and positive, light and darkness, life and death—the balance of nature.

Eight festivals, or sabbats (four major and four lesser), are celebrated by witches each year. Contrary to the image of the witches' sabbat that many imagine, it is not a time when witches gather together to perform magick, cast spells, or concoct all sorts of weird potions. Magick is seldom, if ever, practiced at a sabbat. The witches' sabbat is a religious ceremony deriving from ancient pagan festivals celebrating the change of the seasons. It is a time of dancing, singing, feasting, and honoring the Horned God and the Goddess of Fertility.

The four major sabbats are:

Candlemas: February 2nd
Beltane: May 1st
Lammas: August 1st
Samhain: October 31st

The four lesser sabbats are:

Vernal (Spring) Equinox Sabbat
Summer Solstice Sabbat
Autumnal Equinox Sabbat
Winter Solstice Sabbat (Yule)

Magick is a force that combines psychic energy with will to produce "supernatural" effects, cause change to occur in conformity, and control events in nature. It increases the flow of divinity and can be used for constructive purposes as well as destructive. The actual power of the magick is the same in the practice of black magick as it is in white magick. The direction of evil or good is determined by the practitioner.

Many witches use the old spelling of the word magick with the "k" at the end. This is done to distinguish the magick practiced by witches from the magic of theatrical stage conjuring and sleight of hand. Magick is a powerful tool. It is serious business and should never be taken lightly or abused. It is an important part of witchcraft, although secondary to the worship of the God and the Goddess.

Just as there are many different traditions of witchcraft, there exist many different systems of magick, such as folk magick (conjure, hoodoo, rootwork, etc.), ceremonial (also known as ritual magick or high magick), natural magick, chaos magick, sex magick, and more. Choosing the right form (or forms) of magick to practice depends entirely upon a witch's personal preferences. Some witches and magicians devote their entire lives to the study and practice of only one form of magick while others experiment and practice different types. It is up to the individual.

Magick is the science of the secrets of nature, and in order to work it properly, a witch must work in harmony with the laws of nature and the psyche. Bathing in salted water and cleansing the inner body by fasting for one whole day before performing a magick ritual is sometimes necessary. To be able to produce power, the physical body must be kept in a healthy condition.

The moon in each of her phases is the most essential element of magick.

Constructive magick, positive incantations, and spells that increase things are always performed during a waxing moon. Destructive magick, negative incantations, and all spells that decrease things are performed during a waning moon. Working during the proper time of the moon, conviction, concentration, and visualization of the end result are the secrets of all successful magick!

Whichever type of magick a witch chooses to practice, she or he should always bear in mind the Wiccan Rede, the main tenet of witchcraft: "AN IT HARM NONE, DO WHAT THOU WILT." Be free to do as you please, just as long as you bring harm upon no one—including yourself. Some witches believe if you do evil unto others, the evil will return to you threefold in the same lifetime. This same karmic law of retribution applies whenever you do something good—three times the good will come back to you.

MAY THE GOD AND GODDESS
PRESERVE THE CRAFT
SO MOTE IT BE!

1

Sabbat Feasts

THE FOUR MAJOR SABBATS
Candlemas—February 2
Beltane—May 1
Lammas—August 1
Samhain—October 31

THE FOUR LESSER SABBATS
Vernal Equinox
Summer Solstice
Autumnal Equinox
Winter Solstice/Yule

Candlemas: The Feast of Lights February 2nd

Candlemas, also known as Imbolc, Brigid's Day, and
Lady Day, was originally a pagan fire festival associated
with Brigid, a fertility goddess of pre-Christian Ireland. It
is traditionally celebrated from sunset on the first day of
February to sunset on the following day.

It is a sabbat that celebrates light, fertility, and new be-
ginnings. Many modern witches also regard it as a time
for self-blessings, dedications, and inner journeys for
Divine inspiration. Candles are traditionally placed in
windows to welcome the rebirth of spring, and the
"sweeping out of the old" is symbolized by the sweeping
of the magick circle with a besom, or witches' broom.
Other activities include household purification rituals,
the lighting of hearth fires (especially using Yule greenery), and the making of Brigid's crosses from rushes or
stalks of wheat, which are then hung in the home as
charms to protect against fires and to invite the blessings
of the Goddess.

Gerina's recipes for a Candlemas feast consist of Pot-
latch Stew, Sybil Leeks, Gypsy Tea, Fertility Bread, Poppy
Seed Cake, and Sage Wine.

POTLATCH STEW

3 pounds of beef stew meat (or beef kabob)
2 tablespoons sunflower oil
5 potatoes
4 medium carrots
3 medium onions
3 medium turnips
4 celery stalks
6–8 cups beef broth
½ cup barley
7 chickweed leaves
¼ cup young tops of stinging or great nettle salt
    and pepper
1 teaspoon thyme

Remove fat from beef and cut meat into small square pieces. Heat oil in large skillet. Add the meat and brown over medium heat. Remove from skillet and put meat into a large stew pot. Wash, peel and dice the potatoes, carrots, onions, turnips and celery stalks. Add the vegetables to the stew pot. Next, add the beef broth, barley, chickweed, nettle, salt, pepper and thyme. Stir together well and bring to a boil. Reduce heat, cover pot and let it simmer 2–2½ hours, stirring occasionally, until beef is tender.

SYBIL LEEKS

3 bunches of thinly sliced leeks
3 cups chopped celery
3 onions, chopped
1 cup sliced fresh mushrooms
1 cup chicken broth
1 cup cooked wild rice
¼ cup finely chopped chives
salt and pepper

Carefully wash the white part of the leeks, discarding the coarse green stalks. Split the leeks lengthwise and rinse out the sand between the layers. Put the leeks, celery, onions and mushrooms in a large saucepan with one cup of broth. Bring to a boil over medium-high heat. Cover; reduce heat and simmer until the vegetables are tender, 15–20 minutes. Stir in the cooked wild rice, chopped chives and some salt and pepper to taste. Serve hot.

GYPSY TEA

2 oranges
3 lemons
13 cloves
1 tablespoon ground allspice
½ cinnamon stick
3 tablespoons black tea
2 quarts boiling water
1¼ cup sugar

Squeeze juice from oranges and lemons; set juice aside. Remove rinds and put in a large container. Add cloves, allspice, cinnamon stick and tea. Pour boiling water over the tea mixture and let it stand for about 10 minutes. Strain and then return liquid to container. Stir in the orange juice, lemon juice and sugar. (Gypsy tea may be served either hot or over crushed ice.)

Fertility Bread

(recipe for two 9 × 5-inch loaves)

½ cup lukewarm water
1 package active dry yeast
1 teaspoon sugar
2 cups goat's milk
½ cup dark molasses
1 tablespoon dried yarrow
6 tablespoons butter
2 teaspoons salt
½ cup sunflower seeds
2 cups regular rolled oats
4½ cups flour

Pour the water into a small bowl and sprinkle the yeast and sugar over it. Let it stand for three minutes and then stir well. Set in a warm place for 20–30 minutes, until the mixture doubles in size. Combine the milk, molasses, yarrow, two tablespoons of butter and the salt in a saucepan and cook over medium heat, stirring occasionally, until bubbles start to appear around the edges of the pan. Pour the milk mixture into a deep bowl and set aside to cool to lukewarm.

Add yeast, sunflower seeds and oats to the milk mixture and stir together. Add three cups of the flour, one cup at a time, and continue stirring until the dough can be gathered into a medium-soft ball. Place the ball of dough on a lightly floured surface and knead, pushing the dough down with the heels of your hands, pressing it forward and folding it back on itself. As you knead, sprinkle by the tablespoonful up to two cups more flour over the ball.

Continue kneading for about 15 minutes or until the dough is smooth and elastic. Reshape it into a ball. With a pastry brush, spread two tablespoons of softened butter evenly inside a deep mixing bowl. Place the dough in the bowl and turn it around to butter the entire surface of the dough.

Cover the bowl with a clean kitchen towel and place it in a draft-free area for about 1½ hours or until the dough doubles in size. Brush the remaining two tablespoons of softened butter over the bottoms and sides of two 9 × 5-inch loaf pans. Punch the dough down with a single blow of your fist and divide it in half. Shape each half into a loaf. Place in the pans and brush the top of each loaf with melted butter. Once again cover with a clean kitchen towel and set aside to rise for about 30 minutes. Preheat the oven to 375 degrees. Bake the loaves for 40–45 minutes or until they are light brown.

Turn out on wire racks and cool before serving.

Poppy Seed Cake

1 cup cooking oil
1 cup honey
3 eggs
3 cups whole-wheat flour
1 cup poppy seeds
3½ teaspoons baking soda
1½ cups buttermilk
½ teaspoon salt

Mix all ingredients together. Bake in a preheated 350 degree oven for 40–45 minutes or until done.

SAGE WINE

1 cup fresh sage
½ cup claret or Burgundy wine

Put the fresh sage and the wine into an electric blender and run it on high speed for a few minutes until the sage leaves are pulverized. Return the wine to its original bottle and chill well before drinking.

Beltane: May 1st

Beltane, also known as Walpurgisnacht (Walpurgis Night) and May Day, is an ancient Gaelic fertility festival that celebrates the union of the Goddess and her consort, the Horned God, to create new life. In the words of Selena Fox from Circle Sanctuary, this sabbat "celebrates the height of spring and the flowering of life."

In olden times it was observed with great bonfires on hillsides to light the way for summer, feasts, visits to sacred wells, and special rituals designed to protect humans as well as their crops and livestock. All candles and hearth fires would be extinguished and then relit with burning torches from the sacred Beltane bonfire. Food or milk would be left on the doorstep or at the base of a tree as an offering to the faerie folk.

One of the many pagan customs and traditions that have filtered down through time is the maypole dance, which is performed around a tall wooden pole decorated with flowers or greenery and hung with bright colored ribbons that are woven into complex patterns by the dancers.

Gerina's recipes for a Beltane feast consist of Beltane Barley Casserole, Salmagundi Pentagram, Spring Salad, Witches' Honey Bread, May Day Pudding, and Merry May Punch.

BELTANE BARLEY CASSEROLE

½ cup butter
2 cups barley
½ cup sliced fresh mushrooms
2 chopped onions
½ cup peas
4 cups chicken broth
½ cup pine nuts

Melt butter in a skillet and saute the barley, stirring frequently until golden. Turn into a greased three-quart casserole. Stir in the mushrooms, onions and peas and three cups of the chicken broth. Bake in a preheated 350 degree oven for one hour. Stir in the pine nuts and the remaining cup of broth. Cover and bake for another 1½ hours.

SALMAGUNDI PENTAGRAM

1 large head lettuce
1 cup grated cheddar cheese
25–30 raw onion rings
13 chopped hard-boiled eggs
Salt and pepper
Crushed rosemary
Herb Salad Dressing (see the next page)
3 pounds chopped cooked beef

Wash and place the lettuce leaves on a large circular dish. Sprinkle with grated cheddar cheese. (Other grated cheeses may be substituted, if desired.) Arrange the onion rings over the lettuce to form a circle around the inside edges of the plate. Place bits of chopped hard boiled eggs in the middle of each onion ring. Season lightly with salt and pepper and crushed rosemary. Next, arrange the beef in the center of the plate to form a star symbol with all five points touching the circle of onion rings. (You may arrange the beef to form other magickal or astrological symbols, if you prefer.) Chill and serve with herb salad dressing.

Herb Salad Dressing

2 egg yolks
1 tablespoon cider vinegar
½ teaspoon salt
½ teaspoon basil
2 tablespoons chopped chives
1 teaspoon parsley
¼ teaspoon tarragon
1 cup safflower oil

Put egg yolks, vinegar, salt and herbs in a small bowl and beat until well blended. Add the oil one teaspoon at a time, beating vigorously after each addition until all of the oil has been used. (If the dressing should separate, beat in slowly and thoroughly either one egg yolk, one tablespoon of cold water or a bit of mayonnaise.) Cover and store in the refrigerator.

Spring Salad

Cattails (young stems)
Tomatoes
Cucumbers
Radishes
Chives
Pigweed leaves
Water cress
Comfrey leaves (young and tender)
Dandelion leaves
Wild mustard leaves
Sorrel
Marigold flowers and stems
Sunflower seeds

Cut cattail stems 10–12 inches from the root and peel off the outer skin. (Save the roots for stew!) Chop into small pieces. Wash and cut tomatoes, cucumbers, radishes and chives into small chunks. Tear leaves into bite-size pieces. Place all ingredients in a large salad bowl. Toss lightly and serve with an herbal dressing.

WITCHES' HONEY BREAD

1½ cups buttermilk
1 cup honey
¼ cup molasses
2 teaspoons baking soda
1 teaspoon salt
1½ cups whole-wheat flour
1 cup white flour
½ cup raisins

Mix together the buttermilk, honey, molasses, baking soda and salt. In a separate bowl, combine the whole-wheat and white flour and add to the buttermilk mixture. Stir in the raisins and pour the batter into a greased 9 × 5-inch loaf pan. Bake the bread for one hour in a 350 degree oven. Turn the loaf out, inverted, on a wire rack to cool.

MAY DAY PUDDING

1 teaspoon and 4 tablespoons softened butter
2 eggs
6 cups milk
1½ teaspoon tansy
4 finely chopped sweet cicely leaves
½ cup dark molasses
¼ cup sugar
¼ teaspoon baking soda
¼ teaspoon salt
1 cup yellow corn meal

Preheat oven to 350 degrees. With a pastry brush, spread one teaspoon of butter over the bottom and sides of a two-quart baking dish. Set aside. In a four to five quart saucepan, beat the eggs with a wire whisk until they are well mixed. Stirring constantly with the whisk, add four cups of the milk, tansy, sweet cicely leaves, molasses, sugar, baking soda and salt. Simmer over medium heat, stirring until the molasses and sugar dissolve. Pour in the corn meal very slowly, stirring constantly to keep the mixture smooth. Cook uncovered, stirring occasionally, until the pudding is thick. Beat in the four tablespoons of butter and remove from heat. Pour in the remaining two cups of milk, beating constantly. Pour the pudding into the buttered baking dish and bake for one hour. Reduce the oven temperature to 300 degrees and continue to bake for about four more hours until the May Day pudding is firm.

MERRY MAY PUNCH

2 cups sweet woodruff (leaves and blossoms)
1 quart sweet wine
1 pint wild strawberries
½ cup sugar
Grated peel and juice of 1 lime

Steep the sweet woodruff leaves and blossoms in the wine for three hours on low heat. Cool. Wash and hull the strawberries. Crush and combine them with the wine, sugar, grated lime peel and lime juice. Cover and chill for several hours. Strain liquid and discard the pulp. Fill a large punch bowl with crushed ice and pour the punch over the ice. Add some more sweet woodruff blossoms to the punch just before serving.

Lammas: August Eve

Lammas, or Lughnasadh, is a sabbat that celebrates the beginning of the harvest season and honors the spirit of the grain fields. It was celebrated by the ancient Druids to pay homage to Lugh, an Irish deity corresponding to the pan-Celtic god Lugus.

In olden times it inspired great gatherings that included plenty of feasting, matchmaking, ritual athletic contests, visits to holy wells or sacred springs, and religious ceremonies that traditionally included an offering of the first agricultural produce of the harvest and the slaughtering of sacred bulls.

Gerina's recipes for a Lammas feast consist of Chicken-Barley Magique, Mumbo Gumbo, Erbe Salade, Cranberry Muffins, Sabbat Cakes, Nectar of the Gods,. and Salem Brown Bread.

CHICKEN-BARLEY MAGIQUE

1¾ pounds boneless skinless chicken breast
  (cooked and shredded)
2 tablespoons olive oil
2½ cups white mushrooms (sliced)
1½ cups chopped celery
1½ cups chopped carrots
1 large yellow onion (chopped)
2 cloves garlic (minced)
6 cups chicken stock or broth
¾ cup pearl barley (uncooked)
2 bay leaves
1 tsp dried sage
½ teaspoon of rosemary
½ teaspoon of thyme
½ teaspoon of marjoram
Salt and pepper, to taste
¼ cup fresh parsley (chopped)

Heat the olive oil in a large pot over medium heat. Add the mushrooms, celery, carrots and onion, and sauté for three to four minutes. Add the minced garlic cloves and sauté for an additional thirty seconds. Stir in the chicken stock or broth, barley, bay leaves, sage, rosemary, thyme and marjoram, and season with salt and pepper to taste. Bring the mixture to a boil and then reduce heat to low, cover and simmer until the barley is tender, about one hour. Stir in the chicken and parsley and serve warm.

Mumbo Gumbo

3 ounces lean salt pork, diced into ¼ inch bits with
   the rind removed
5 onions, peeled and chopped
1 minced green pepper
1½ cups okra
2 cups corn kernels
4 peeled and diced potatoes
salt and pepper (to taste)
2 cups water
½ cup marigold flowers
3 finely chopped rue leaves
1 cup milk
1 cup light cream

In a heavy three-to-four quart casserole, fry the salt pork over medium heat, turning the bits frequently with a spoon until they are crisp and brown.

Transfer the pork bits to paper towels to drain thoroughly. Add the onions, green pepper and okra to the fat remaining in the casserole and cook for 10 minutes, stirring frequently, until the onions are soft and golden brown. Stir in the corn kernels, diced potatoes, salt, pepper and water. Bring to a boil over high heat. Reduce the heat to low and simmer partially covered until the potatoes are soft but still intact. Next, add the reserved pork bits, marigold flowers, rue leaves, milk and cream and cook for 10 minutes, stirring constantly. Serve hot.

ERBE SALADE

Salad burnet leaves
3 chopped rue leaves
Borage stalks, peeled and cut into chunks
Chopped chives
Good King Henry leaves
Lovage stalks
5 tomatoes, cut into small pieces
Herb-seasoned croutons
3 cups pitted and chopped green olives
Herbal salad dressing

Rinse all leaves, stalks and vegetables under cold running water; drain in colander. After drying, transfer to a large salad bowl. Tear leaves into small bite-size pieces. Add the croutons and mix together well. Pour the herbal dressing over the salad and toss lightly.

GERINA'S CRANBERRY MUFFINS

4 tablespoons softened butter
1 cup fresh cranberries
2¾ cup flour
¾ cup sugar
4 teaspoons baking powder
½ teaspoon salt
1 cup milk
1 lightly beaten egg

Preheat oven to 400 degrees. Combine the flour, sugar, baking powder and salt and sift into a deep mixing bowl. Stirring constantly with a big spoon, pour in the milk. Stir in the egg and butter. Add the cranberries and continue to stir until all of the ingredients are well combined. Ladle batter into buttered muffin-tin cups, filling each about ⅔ full. Bake for 30 minutes or until the muffins are brown and a toothpick inserted in the center comes out clean.

SABBAT CAKES

1½ cups rolled oats
1½ cups flour
4 tablespoons sugar
5 tablespoons dark brown sugar
½ teaspoon baking soda
½ teaspoon salt
12 tablespoons butter, chilled and cut into ½-inch
  bits
2 tablespoons vanilla extract
4–6 tablespoons cold water

Combine the oats, flour, sugar, brown sugar, baking soda and salt in a deep mixing bowl and stir until well mixed. Drop in the butter bits and stir the oat and flour mixture together with the butter until it looks like flakes of coarse meal. Pour the vanilla extract and four tablespoons of cold water over the mixture, toss together lightly and gather the dough into a ball. (Add up to two more tablespoons of cold water, drop by drop, if the dough begins to crumble.) Wrap the dough in wax paper and refrigerate for at least 30 minutes. On a lightly floured surface, roll the dough out into a rough rectangle about 1/8 of an inch thick. With a stick and a sharp knife, cut the dough into two-inch triangles. Arrange the sabbat cakes about an inch apart on a large buttered baking sheet and bake in a preheated 350 degree oven for 20 minutes, until they are golden brown and firm. Cool on wire racks before serving. This recipe makes 40 two-inch triangular cakes.

NECTAR OF THE GODS

2 cups apricot nectar
1½ cups fruit salad
1 cup sliced bananas
1 cup pineapple juice
1 cup chopped pineapple
½ cup maraschino cherry juice
2 ounces rum

Mix all ingredients together in a large punch bowl. Chill for several hours and add crushed ice just before serving.

Salem Brown Bread

2 cups buttermilk
¾ cup dark molasses
1 cup raisins
1 cup rye flour
1 cup whole wheat flour
1 cup yellow corn meal
¾ teaspoon baking soda
1 teaspoon salt
1 tablespoon softened butter

In a deep bowl, beat the buttermilk and molasses together vigorously with a spoon. Stir in the raisins. Combine the rye flour, whole wheat flour, corn meal, baking soda and salt and sift them into the buttermilk mixture one cup at a time, stirring well after each addition. Butter the bottom and sides of two 2½ cup tin cans. Pour the batter into the cans, dividing it evenly between them. The batter should fill each can to within about one inch of the top.

Cover each can loosely with a circle of buttered wax paper and then with a larger circle of aluminum foil. The foil should be puffed like the top of a French chef's hat, allowing an inch of space above the top edge of the cans so the batter can rise as it is steamed. Tie the wax paper and foil in place with string. Stand the cans on a rack in a large pot and pour in enough boiling water to come about ¾ of the way up the sides of the cans. Bring the water to a boil. Cover the pot tightly and reduce the heat. Steam the bread for two hours and 15 minutes. Remove the foil and paper from the cans at once, and turn the bread out.

Samhain: October 31st

Samhain, also known as Halloween, is the ancient Celtic/ Druid New Year and the most important of all the four major sabbats. It is a sacred festival that marks the end of the Goddess-ruled summer and welcomes the beginning of the God-ruled winter. Traditionally celebrated from sunset on the last day of October to sunset of November 1st, it has long been regarded as the time of year when the veil separating the world of the living from the world of the dead is at its thinnest. Many witches believe Samhain is a night when spirits of dead friends and loved ones return to rejoice, briefly, with the living. Rites to honor the deceased are performed by covens and solitaries alike.

Along with the carving of jack-o'-lanterns (which were, at one time, believed to possess the power to scare away malevolent entities), scrying (crystal-gazing), rune casting, and seances are traditions also associated with this sabbat.

Gerina's recipes for a Samhain feast consist of Partridge Casserole, Baked Hominy (Country Witch style), Marsh Marigolds with Mushroom Sauce, Wild Berry Bread, Magick Pumpkin Squares, and Samhain Cider.

PARTRIDGE CASSEROLE

12 partridges
½ cup butter
6 cups chopped celery
2½ teaspoons salt
2 teaspoons pepper
4 tablespoons lemon juice
2 cups mayonnaise or salad dressing
3 cups grated cheddar cheese
1 cup seasoned bread crumbs

Wash and dry partridges. Cut each in half and sprinkle with salt. Melt butter in large skillet over medium heat. Add partridges; sauté well on all sides. Add two or three cups of water to skillet. Cover and simmer for one hour or until tender. (Add more water to skillet if evaporation occurs while simmering.) Take out partridges, remove bones and chop meat into small chunks. Combine with celery, salt, pepper, lemon juice, mayonnaise, cheddar cheese, breadcrumbs and poultry seasoning. Toss lightly and turn into a large greased casserole. Sprinkle with extra cheese and bake in a preheated 450 degree oven for 20 minutes or until the cheese bubbles.

Baked Hominy (Country Witch Style)

2 cups hominy
2 quarts boiling salted water
2 eggs
2 cups milk
2 tablespoons brown sugar

Boil hominy in salted water over medium heat for one hour, stirring occasionally. Remove from heat and cool. Preheat oven to 400 degrees. Stir eggs, milk and brown sugar into hominy. Turn into a greased three-quart casserole and bake for about 30 minutes.

MARSH MARIGOLDS WITH MUSHROOM SAUCE

6 cups marsh marigold leaves
½ cup sliced fresh mushrooms
4 tablespoons butter
½ cup whole wheat flour
1 cup milk
pinch of salt and pepper
2 tablespoons chopped parsley

Wash and then steam the heart-shaped leaves of the marsh marigolds (or cowslips) for 15–20 minutes. Arrange the leaves on a large serving platter. To make the sauce, sauté mushrooms in butter. Add flour and stir in milk.

Season with salt, pepper and parsley. Pour the mushroom sauce over the steamed leaves and serve.

Wild Berry Bread

6 tablespoons softened butter, cut into 1/2-inch bits
2 cups flour
½ cup raspberries
½ cup blackberries
1 cup blueberries
1 cup sugar
1½ teaspoons baking powder
½ teaspoon baking soda
½ teaspoon salt
1 egg, lightly beaten
1 tablespoon finely grated orange peel
½ cup orange juice

Wash the berries under cold running water and pat them dry with paper towels. Crush the berries; set aside. Combine the flour, sugar, baking powder, baking soda and salt and sift into a deep bowl. Add the butter bits and, with your fingertips, rub the butter and dry ingredients together until they become like flakes of coarse meal. Mix in the egg, orange peel and orange juice and add the berries while continuing to stir until all of the ingredients are thoroughly combined. Spoon the batter into a buttered 9 × 5-inch loaf pan, spreading it and smoothing the top with a spatula. Bake in a preheated 350 degree oven for 1½ hours or until the top is golden brown and a toothpick inserted in the center of the loaf comes out clean. Turn the loaf out onto a wire rack to cool.

MAGICK PUMPKIN SQUARES

½ cup butter
1½ cups honey
2 eggs
1 cup buttermilk
2 cups pumpkin, boiled and mashed or canned
2 cups whole wheat flour
½ teaspoon salt
1 teaspoon baking soda
2 teaspoons cinnamon
1 teaspoon nutmeg
1 teaspoon cloves
½ teaspoon allspice
2 cups uncooked oats
1 cup quartered dates
1 cup crushed walnuts

Beat butter, eggs, honey, buttermilk and pumpkin. Add flour, salt, baking soda, spices and oats. Mix well. Add the dates and nuts and stir together. Grease a 9 × 9-inch pan and spread batter evenly. Bake in a preheated 375 degree oven for 35–40 minutes or until done. Remove from pan, cool and cut into small squares.

SAMHAIN CIDER

2 quarts apple cider
½ teaspoon cinnamon
½ teaspoon nutmeg
¼ teaspoon ginger
½ cup confectioner's sugar
½ cup apricot brandy

In a large pot, combine the apple cider, cinnamon, nutmeg, ginger and sugar. Simmer slowly on low heat for about 15 minutes—do not boil. Add the brandy and serve warm. (Serves 13.)

2

The Esbat and Miscellaneous Witch Recipes

The Esbat

THE ESBAT IS A MONTHLY COVEN MEETING held 13 times a year during each full moon. At the Esbat, witches of the coven chant, exchange ideas, perform special rites, work magick and healing, give thanks and/or request help from the gods. A traditional "Cakes and Wine" or "Cakes and Ale" ceremony also takes place.

Natural snacks like nuts, raisins, fruits (fresh or dried) and home-baked cookies or muffins may also be served at the Esbat in addition to the traditional cakes, wine and ale. "Junk food" snacks that contain artificial flavors, preservatives and unhealthful chemicals are definitely not recommended. Remember: You are what you eat!

The following is a collection of old witches' recipes for foods and wines traditionally served at Esbats and coven meetings: Esbat Cake, Coven Cakes, Acorn Cookies, Salem Shortbread, Graham Bread, Onion Butter (Spread), Witches' Mix, Wild Fennel Muffins, Dandelion Wine, Divination Wine, Mandrake Wine, Sweet Tomato Wine, and Nettle Ale.

Esbat Cake

2¼ cups flour
1½ cups sugar
½ teaspoon salt
1 teaspoon baking powder
1½ teaspoons baking soda
½ teaspoon ground cloves
½ teaspoon crushed coriander seeds
1¼ teaspoon cinnamon
1¼ cups buttermilk
1 egg
½ cup melted butter

Preheat the oven to 350 degrees. In a large mixing bowl, sift together the flour, sugar, salt, baking powder, baking soda, cloves, coriander seeds and cinnamon. Stir in the buttermilk, egg and cooled melted butter and mix well until the batter is smooth. Pour the batter into a greased cake pan and bake for one hour or until a knife inserted in the center of the cake comes out clean.

Place on a rack and cool for at least 20 minutes before unmolding.

COVEN CAKES

1¾ cups oatmeal
¼ teaspoon baking powder
½ teaspoon salt
½ teaspoon cream of tartar
½ teaspoon cinnamon
7 teaspoons sugar
1½ tablespoons melted butter
7 teaspoons hot water

Combine the oatmeal, baking powder, salt, cream of tartar, cinnamon and sugar in a bowl. Stir in the melted butter. Add the hot water, one teaspoon at a time, stirring constantly, until mixture becomes a smooth but firm paste.

Gather the mixture into a ball and place it on a board or tabletop lightly sprinkled with about one-quarter cup of oatmeal. Roll the ball into the oatmeal until it is completely covered with the flakes. Spread another one-quarter cup of oatmeal evenly over the board and roll the ball out into an eight-inch circle one-eighth inch thick with a rolling pin. With a sharp knife, cut the circle into eight pie-shaped wedges. Sprinkle a bit of oatmeal on a baking sheet and with a large spatula, carefully transfer the wedges to the sheet. Bake the coven cakes in the middle of a preheated 350 degree oven for about 15 minutes or until the wedges are light brown. Turn off the oven and open the oven door. Leave the coven cakes in the oven for about five minutes or until they become firm and crisp.

ACORN COOKIES

1¾ cups flour
½ teaspoon salt
½ teaspoon baking soda
1 teaspoon baking powder
1 teaspoon cinnamon
1 teaspoon nutmeg
¼ pound butter
1 teaspoon vanilla
1 cup sugar
2 eggs
1 cup raisins
1½ cup chopped acorns

Sift together the flour, salt, baking soda, baking powder, cinnamon and nutmeg. Set aside. In a large bowl, cream the butter. Add the vanilla and sugar and beat well. Add the eggs and beat until smooth. Gradually add the sifted dry ingredients, beating until thoroughly mixed. Stir in the raisins and acorns. Place well-rounded teaspoonfuls of dough two inches apart on a foil-covered cookie sheet. Bake in a preheated 400 degree oven for 12–15 minutes.

SALEM SHORTBREAD

1 pound softened butter
1 cup sugar
4 cups flour
1½ tablespoons cornstarch
1 egg

Mix the butter and sugar together until creamy. Add the flour and cornstarch and then stir in the egg. Pat onto an ungreased cookie sheet. Smooth with a spatula and prick with a fork. Bake in a preheated 300 degree oven for two hours. Remove from the oven and cut into squares while still hot.

GRAHAM BREAD

1½ cups graham flour
2 cups flour
¾ cup brown sugar
½ cup molasses
2 cups buttermilk
2 teaspoons baking soda
1 teaspoon salt

Mix all ingredients together in a large mixing bowl until well blended. Pour the batter into a greased 9 × 5 × 3-inch loaf pan and bake in a preheated 350 degree oven for 45 minutes or until a knife inserted into the center of the loaf comes out clean.

Onion Butter

5 lbs. onions
water
salt

Peel and quarter the onions. Place them in a large heavy kettle and barely cover them with water. Bring to a boil, then cover and simmer gently for 24 hours, adding more water whenever necessary. After the liquid has concentrated into about 2½ pints of lumpy dark brown "honey," break it up into a paste of uniform consistency. Add salt to taste and continue to simmer uncovered until the final excess liquid evaporates.

Use on homemade bread and biscuits as a delicious spread.

WITCHES' MIX (GRANOLA)

4 cups rolled wheat
1 cup rolled oats
½ cup bran
1 cup chopped nuts
1 cup hulled sunflower seeds
1½ cups shredded coconut
1 cup raisins
½ cup sesame seeds
½ cup oil
1 cup honey
2 teaspoons vanilla extract

Mix together the rolled wheat, oats, bran, chopped nuts, sunflower seeds, coconut, raisins and sesame seeds. Heat the oil, honey and vanilla. Combine with the dry ingredients and mix. Bake on an oiled cookie sheet for 30 minutes in a 375 degree oven, turning frequently.

Wild Fennel Muffins

2 cups flour
4 teaspoons baking powder
¼ teaspoon baking soda
½ teaspoon ground nutmeg
½ teaspoon cinnamon
½ teaspoon salt
4 tablespoons softened butter
¼ cup brown sugar
2 eggs
1 cup sour cream
⅓ cup wild fennel seeds
3 peeled, cored and chopped apples

Combine the flour, baking powder, baking soda, nutmeg, cinnamon and salt. Sift them together in a bowl and then set aside.

Cream the butter and sugar in a deep mixing bowl until the mixture becomes light and fluffy. Beat in the eggs, one at a time. Add one cup of the flour mixture and then beat in one-half cup of the sour cream. Repeat, beating in the remaining flour and then the rest of the cream, and stir until the batter is smooth. Stir in the fennel seeds and chopped apples and spoon the batter into buttered muffin cups, filling each cup almost halfway to the top. Sprinkle fennel seeds on top of each muffin. Insert a slice of apple partway into the top of each muffin, if desired.

Bake in the middle of a preheated 425 degree oven for 15–20 minutes or until the fennel muffins are brown and a toothpick inserted in the centers comes out clean.

Dandelion Wine

3 quarts of dandelion flowers
2 gallons spring water
7 pounds sugar
3 oranges
3 lemons
¼ box of seedless raisins
1 yeast cake (or 1 envelope dry yeast)

(To make Dandelion Wine you will need three quarts of open dandelion flowers, packed tightly with stems removed.)

Cover dandelions in crock with boiling water. Let it stand for three days.

Strain through a colander and discard dandelions. Add the seven pounds of sugar to the liquid. Slice the oranges and lemons, leaving the peels but removing the seeds. Add the fruits to the liquid. Next, add the raisins and stir thoroughly. Boil for 20 minutes and then remove from heat. Let it stand for another 24 hours.

Add the yeast, dissolved in six tablespoons of hot water. Stir and then strain the mixture through a wet muslin or clean dish towel into wine bottles, filling them to the brim. Tie pieces of muslin over the bottle tops or seal with corks. Do not cap bottles too tightly. Small amounts of gas may form and must be allowed to escape.

The wine is ready to drink after fermentation has stopped and no more bubbles appear in the bottles. Store in a dark cool place for up to six months.

DIVINATION WINE

Follow the instructions for dandelion wine, using one quart each of cowslip flowers, dogwood blossoms and rose hips instead of the three quarts of dandelions. Omit the raisins from the recipe.

MANDRAKE WINE

Remove the stems, skins and seeds from 13 medium apples. Boil the apples for about 20 minutes. Drain and mash together with the fully ripe oval lemon-colored fruit of one mandrake (American variety) also known as the May Apple.

CAUTION: Do not use any other part of the mandrake: The fully ripe fruit is edible, but the rest of the plant is *very* poisonous.

Follow the instructions for making dandelion wine, using three quarts of mashed apples and mandrake fruit in place of the dandelions. Omit the raisins from the recipe.

Sweet Tomato Wine

Start by removing the stalks from three quarts of ripe red tomatoes. Cut the tomatoes into small pieces and then mash them well. Drain through a hair-sieve. Season the tomato juice with salt and sugar to taste. Pour into jars and tie pieces of muslin over the tops. Let stand until the fermentation process has ended and there are no more bubbles. Pour off the clear liquid into wine bottles and cork tightly.

Allow the wine to age at least three months in a cellar or other cool, dark place before drinking.

NETTLE ALE

2 gallons young nettles
2½ gallons water
¾ ounce bruised ginger root
4 ounces sarsaparilla
4 pounds malt
2 ounces hops
1½ pounds sugar
1 ounce yeast

Wash the nettles and place them in a large pot. Add 2½ gallons of well water or pure spring water, the ginger root, sarsaparilla, malt and hops. Boil for 15–20 minutes. Remove from heat and strain over 1½ lbs. of sugar. Stir well until the sugar dissolves and then add the yeast. Bottle the ale when it begins to ferment. Seal the bottles with corks and tie down with string. (Note: Nettle ale needs no keeping.)

Miscellaneous Witches' Recipes

13 BEWITCHIN' KITCHEN TIPS

1. A quartz crystal placed on or near the stove when cooking makes food taste better.
2. A pot of basil herb grown in your kitchen keeps the area safe from evil forces and negative spirits.
3. Candles keep their shape better and burn longer when chilled thoroughly in the refrigerator.
4. A witch's kitchen should never be without a lunar calendar or chart showing the phases of the moon and its movement through the wheel of the zodiac.
5. A full moon increases extrasensory perception and is the ideal time to prepare and use potions that increase the psychic abilities.
6. Love philtres and aphrodisiacs should always be prepared during the waxing of the moon.
7. The best time to plant an herb or vegetable garden is when the moon is in Cancer, Scorpio, Libra or Pisces.
8. Homemade magickal incenses, sachets and potpourris become more fragrant if aged several months before used.
9. Homemade incense always should be stored in tightly capped or corked jars.
10. Unlucky influences should be kept away from the kitchen when cooking or preparing magickal recipes, and this is accomplished by stirring in a clockwise direction.
11. An aloe vera plant should be kept in the kitchen, as its juices are an instant cure for minor kitchen burns.
12. Herbal preparations should never be boiled in aluminum vessels, but in only copper, earthenware or Pyrex to avoid contamination of the medicines.

13. Before casting spells or preparing potions, always keep in mind the Wiccan Rede: "Do what ye will an it harm none."

Wiccan Handfasting Cake

1 cup butter
1 cup sugar
½ cup honey
5 eggs
2 cups flour
2 tablespoons grated lemon rind
2½ teaspoons lemon juice
1 teaspoon rosewater
Pinch of basil
6 fresh rose geranium leaves

In a large mixing bowl, cream the butter and sugar until fluffy and light. Add the honey and mix well. Add the eggs, one at a time, beating well after each addition. Gradually add the flour and blend thoroughly with a large wooden spoon following each egg. Stir in the lemon rind, lemon juice, rose water and a pinch of basil—the herb of love. Line the bottom of a greased 9×5×3-inch loaf pan with the rose geranium leaves and then pour in the batter. Bake the cake in a preheated 350 degree oven for one hour and 15 minutes. Remove from oven when done and let it stand on a rack for 20 minutes before un-molding. Sprinkle powdered sugar on top of the hand-fasting cake just before serving.

Yule Cake

3 sticks softened butter
3 tablespoons softened butter
1¼ cups and 2 tablespoons flour
¾ cup chopped candied cherries
1¼ cups raisins
1¼ cups dried currants
1½ cups sugar
7 eggs
1 teaspoon ground allspice
1 tablespoon salt
1 cup chopped walnuts

Preheat oven to 300 degrees. Using a pastry brush, coat the sides and bottom of a 9 × 3-inch springform cake pan with the three tablespoons of the softened butter. Sprinkle the two tablespoons of flour into the pan. Tip pan from side to side to spread the flour evenly, then turn it upside down and give it a whack on the bottom to remove the excess flour. Combine the cherries, raisins and currants in a bowl, add one-quarter cup of the flour and stir the fruit with a spoon, coating the pieces evenly. Set aside. In a large bowl, cream three-quarter pounds of softened butter, the sugar and two additional tablespoons of the flour together by working them against the sides of the bowl until they are light and fluffy. Beat in the eggs, one at a time, and then gradually beat in the rest of the flour, the allspice and the salt. Combine the nuts with the fruit mixture and add to the batter, one-half cup at a time, beating well after each addition. Pour the batter into the cake pan, spreading it out with a spatula. Bake in the middle of the oven for about 1½ hours or until the top of the Yule cake is golden and a toothpick inserted in the center of the cake comes out clean. Make sure the cake is completely cool before removing it from the pan.

Passion Potpourri

2 ounces violet
2 ounces orris root
1 ounce lovage
½ ounce rose leaf
½ ounce rose petal
1 ounce rosemary
1 ounce tonka bean
½ ounce lemon leaf

Cut and collect the herbs on a dry morning after the dew has dried. Tie the herbs together securely with a red string and hang them to dry in an attic or other warm, dark, airy place. Remove the string after the herbs are dry and brittle, and break them into large coarse pieces. (It is important that the herbs be completely dry, otherwise mold will develop and ruin the potpourri.) Stir the ingredients together with a large wooden spoon and then place in a large glass jar, bottle or jug and seal with a tight-fitting lid. Keep the potpourri in a cool dark place for three months, removing the lid and stirring the contents with a wooden spoon at least once a week.

PASSION APHRODISIAC—Place a handful of the passion potpourri into a nylon stocking, muslin or cheesecloth bag and add to your bath water to increase sexual power.

PASSION SACHET—On a night of the waxing moon, place one ounce of the passion potpourri in a silk handkerchief. Fill your mind with romantic thoughts as you gather together the corners of the handkerchief and tie them securely with a piece of red velvet. Carry the sachet of passion potpourri with you at all times during the day to help guide a lover into your life. At night, place the sachet under your pillow before going to sleep.

PASSION VISION INCENSE—Burn a pinch of the passion potpourri on a hot charcoal block as a magickal incense to receive a psychic vision of your future lovemate.

FRANKINCENSE

2 tablespoons powdered frankincense
1 tablespoon powdered orris root
1 teaspoon powdered clove
1 tablespoon lemon oil

Combine and mix together the frankincense, orris root and clove. Stir the lemon oil through the mixture. Put it in a clean glass jar, seal or cork tightly and keep in a dark, cool place for two or three months before using.

Frankincense is an excellent incense to use when performing healing magick. It can also be consecrated and burned on a hot charcoal block as an altar incense to honor the Horned God and Mother Goddess.

GODDESS INCENSE

½ ounce ground rose petals
½ dram cypress oil
½ dram olive oil
½ ounce powdered white willow bark

Mix together all ingredients and burn on a hot charcoal block to honor the Goddess.

GOOD OMEN INCENSE

5 rose petals
1½ ounce myrrh
1 ounce dragon's blood
½ ounce sassafras
½ ounce orange blossoms
½ ounce juniper
½ ounce sage
½ dram frankincense oil

Mix all ingredients together and burn on a hot charcoal block to attract good luck.

Kyphi Isis Incense

½ ounce benzoin
½ ounce cinnamon
½ ounce frankincense
½ ounce galangal
1 ounce myrrh
3 drops lotus oil
3 drops honey

Using your hands, mix together the benzoin, cinnamon, frankincense, galangal and myrrh in a large nonmetallic bowl. Add the lotus oil and honey and mix thoroughly. Cover the bowl tightly with a plastic wrap and let it sit undisturbed for two weeks in a dark place.

With a mortar and pestle, grind the ingredients into a fine powder and burn on a hot charcoal block as a magickal incense or to invoke ancient Egyptian deities.

WITCHES' FLYING OINTMENT

¼ cup lard
½ teaspoon clove oil
1 teaspoon chimney soot
¼ teaspoon cinquefoil
¼ teaspoon mugwort
¼ teaspoon thistle
¼ teaspoon vervain
½ teaspoon tincture of benzoin

In a small saucepan, heat the lard over low flame until it is melted. Add the clove oil, chimney soot, cinquefoil, mugwort, thistle and vervain to the lard base and mix together well. Add the benzoin as a natural preservative, stir and then simmer for 10–15 minutes. Strain through a cheesecloth into a small fireproof container and store in refrigerator or a cool dark place. Anoint your body with the flying ointment prior to astral projection.

Old-Fashioned Witch Soap

4 pounds lard
13 ounces lye (1 can)
5 cups cold water
1 tablespoon lavender oil
1 tablespoon patchouli oil
1 cup fresh strawberry juice
¼ cup dried soap bark herb (optional)

In a large enamel or iron kettle, melt the lard over very low heat. (IMPORTANT: Never use aluminum pots or utensils when working with soap containing lye!) In a separate iron or enamel pot, stir together the lye and the water. Heat until small bubbles begin to appear—do not boil.

Remove from the heat and slowly pour the lye solution into the lard. With a big wooden spoon, stir in the lavender and patchouli oils, the strawberry juice and soap bark herb. Simmer for about 30 minutes, stirring frequently. Pour into two-inch deep greased enamel or glass pans and allow to cool overnight. Cut the soap into squares and leave in the pans for at least three days before removing. Place the soap bars on waxed paper and allow them to "age" in a draft-free area for four to six weeks before using.

3

Candle Crafting

CANDLEMAKING IS AN ANCIENT CRAFT that is practiced by witches who prefer working with their own homemade candles rather than the store-bought ones. Candles that are made by hand absorb the witch's own psychic energies and thereby are more magickally powerful than those that are mass-produced in factories.

To make your own candles you will need: equal parts paraffin and pure beeswax (amount depending upon the number you plan to make), a double boiler, wicking and candle molds. These items can be easily found in most hobby and craft stores as well as candle shops. Waxed milk cartons, muffin cups and metal cans make perfect (and inexpensive) candle molds, as do plastic and glass bottles of various sizes and shapes.

Cut the candle wicking to fit the size of the mold, allowing one extra inch of wick above the top of the mold. Attach a nut or screw to the bottom of the wick as a weight and then insert into the center of the mold.

Cut the paraffin into small pieces and place them in the top of the double boiler. (A large tin can placed in a pan of boiling water may be used in place of the double boiler.) Add the pure beeswax to the paraffin and melt over low heat. Do not try to melt the wax directly over fire. Scent with oil of cloves, lavender, lemon oil, mint, rose, sage or any other aromatic herb oils. For colored candles, melt a colored wax crayon in the paraffin.

After the paraffin and beeswax have been melted down, slowly pour into the candle molds. As the wax cools, a depression will form in the middle of the candle's top near the wick. Refill the depression with more melted wax until the mold is level.

Remove the candles from their molds only after the wax has dried and hardened thoroughly.

Dressing the Candle

Before using a candle in a magickal ceremony, it is recommended that the candle be dressed—or anointed—with a small amount of oil (as below).

Using your bare hands, rub the oil into the wax starting at the middle of the candle and working your way up to the top. Start again, this time at the middle of the candle and work your way down to the bottom to complete the anointing ritual.

This ancient practice of candle-oiling helps to put your psychic vibrations into the candle, magnetizing it and transforming it into an extension of your mind power.

CANDLE ANOINTING OIL

1 cup rose petals
1 cup violets
1 cup water
1 cup olive oil
1 tablespoon clove oil
2 teaspoons powdered cinnamon
1 tablespoon powdered myrrh
¼ cup wild fennel seeds

Gather the rose petals and violets at sunrise. Place them in a clean ceramic crock. Cover with water (fresh rain water, preferably) and let crock sit in a sunny location for three days until an oily film (the essential oil of the flowers) is seen floating on top of the water.

Remove the oil from the water by carefully absorbing it into a small cotton ball. Squeeze out the oil into a clean, long-necked glass bottle. Add the olive and clove oils, and gently swirl the bottle in a clockwise direction to slowly agitate the oils. Next, add the cinnamon, myrrh and fennel seeds.

Seal the bottle tightly and store it in a dark, cool place. After four weeks, strain the oil through a cheesecloth and use for candle anointing rituals.

Color

The color of the candle is very important when it comes to performing magick for each color possesses a different vibration and attracts different spiritual influences. (See "Evocation of Spirits" in Chapter 5—Spellcasting.)

Each of the 12 signs of the zodiac is also ruled by its own color, and when casting horoscopes or working zodiac-related magick, the colors of the candles used should correspond to the proper zodiacal color:

AQUARIUS: Light blue
PISCES: Aquamarine
ARIES: Red
TAURUS: Green
GEMINI: Yellow or silver
CANCER: White
LEO: Gold
VIRGO: Gray
LIBRA: Royal blue
SCORPIO: Black or red
SAGITTARIUS: Dark blue or purple
CAPRICORN: Black or dark brown

During the four major witches' sabbats, the following colored candles should be burned: brown for Candlemas, dark green for Beltane, yellow for Lammas and orange or black for Samhain.

Candle magick should never be performed in the dark of the moon—the three days preceding a new moon. A waxing moon is the proper time to perform spells that attract, and the waning moon is the correct time to perform spells that banish.

Candles that are used when working black magick

should *never* be reused for white magick spells as the negative vibrations of the candle will interfere with the magick and possibly reverse the effects of the spell.

Bayberry Candles

The wax of bayberries produces pleasant smelling candles that can be used for healing, spiritual purification, protection or increasing the powers of the psyche.

To obtain the bayberry wax, boil at least 10 cups of berries in a large kettle of pure water until the bayberry wax floats to the surface. (Always use spring, rain or well water. Never use water from the tap when crafting candles for magickal use.)

Remove from heat and allow to cool for one to two hours. After the wax has hardened, remove it from the kettle and combine it with paraffin to make candles.

Magick Herb Candles

Herbs are an extremely important part of candle crafting for each herb possesses a different magickal property.

When preparing candles for spells, a small amount of the appropriate powdered herb should be added to the melted wax before pouring it into the candle mold. This provides the candle with the proper magickal energy needed for spellcasting.

The following is a list of common witches' herbs and their magickal properties:

ACACIA: Divination.

ADDER'S TONGUE: Divination.

ANGELICA: Exorcism, healing and protection against evil influences.

AVENS: Soul purification.

BASIL: Exorcism, love spells and protection against evil influences.

BAY: Clairvoyance, healing, good luck and protection against evil influences.

BERGAMOT: Prosperity.

CAMPHOR: Divination.

CATNIP: Love spells.

CARNATION: Psychic healing.

CEDAR: Healing, prosperity and sanctification.

CHAMOMILE: Sleep potions.

CINNAMON: Clairvoyance, healing and love spells.

CINQUEFOIL: Prosperity.

CLOVES: Divination, exorcism, love and spiritual purification.

CLOVER: Anti-sorcery, counterspells and protection against evil influences.

CORIANDER: Love spells.

DILL: Anti-sorcery and protection against evil influences.

DRAGON'S BLOOD: Exorcism and love spells.

ELDER: Aphrodisiac, love spells and prosperity.

FENNEL: Healing and purification.

FERN: Exorcism and spells to attract rain.

FRANKINCENSE: Consecration, divination, exorcism, healing, love spells and spiritual purification.

GARDENIA: Healing and love spells.

GARLIC: Exorcism, protection against evil influences and purification.

GINGER: Aphrodisiacs and love spells.

GINSENG: Aphrodisiacs, love spells, and spiritual purification.

HAWTHORNE FLOWERS: Clairvoyance and divination.

HAZEL: Aphrodisiacs and love spells.

HONEYSUCKLE: Divination.

HOPS: Healing and sleep potions.

HOREHOUND: Exorcism and healing.

JASMINE: Aphrodisiacs and love spells.

JUNIPER: Aphrodisiacs, exorcism, healing, love spells and protection against evil influences.

LAVENDER: Aphrodisiacs and love spells.

LEMON BALM: Healing and love spells.

LEMON GRASS: Divination.

LEMON VERBENA: Aphrodisiacs, clairvoyance and prophetic dreams.

LILAC: Exorcism.

LOTUS FLOWERS: Fertility, healing, inner peace and meditation.

LOVAGE: Aphrodisiacs and love spells.

MACE: Divination.

MALLOW: Exorcism.

MANDRAKE ROOT: Aphrodisiac, cursing enemies, love spells, protection against evil influences and spells to increase psychic powers.

MARIGOLD: Anti-sorcery and psychic visions.

MARJORAM: Prophetic dreams and protection against evil influences.

MINT: Exorcism and healing.

MISTLETOE: Exorcism.

MUGWORT: Astral projection, clairvoyance, divination, prophetic dreams, protection against evil influences and spells to increase psychic powers.

MYRRH: Consecration, exorcism, healing and meditation.

MYRTLE: Sleep potions.

NUTMEG: Divination and prosperity.

ORRIS ROOT: Clairvoyance and divination.

PASSIONFLOWER: Sleep potions.

PATCHOULY: Invocation of elemental powers.

PEONY ROOT: Anti-sorcery and protection against evil influences.

PEPPERMINT: Divination and healing.

PINE: Prosperity

ROSE: Divination, healing and love spells.

ROSEMARY: Counterspells, healing, love spells and purification.

RUE: Exorcism and hexing of enemies.

SAFFRON: Love spells.

SANDALWOOD: Consecration, healing and protection against evil influences.

SASSAFRASS: Prosperity.

SERPENTARIA ROOT: Aphrodisiacs and love spells.

SOLOMON'S SEAL: Exorcism.

ST. JOHN'S WORT: Anti-sorcery, exorcism and protection against evil influences.

THISTLE: Exorcism.

THYME: Divination and healing.

TONKA: Love spells and prosperity.

VERVAIN: Anti-sorcery, astral projection and sleep potions.

VIOLET: Healing and love spells.

WILLOW: Healing.

WOOD ALOE: Prosperity.

WOODRUFF: Prosperity.

WORMWOOD: Clairvoyance, divination and good
luck.

YARROW: Divination, exorcism, love spells, prophetic
dreams, protection against evil influences and
spells to increase psychic powers.

YERBA SANTA: Healing.

4

Herbs

Healing Herbs

FOR ALMOST EVERY MALADY that ails the human body, there is a natural herbal remedy, and witches have possessed knowledge of these remedies for many centuries.

The relationship between witchcraft and herbalism goes back a long way. In the old days before medicine or science existed, the simple country witches were the first to bravely experiment with wild-growing plants, and it was not long before they learned of the wonderful, magickal healing qualities found in many flowers, roots, and leaves.

The power to heal wounds and to cure the ill with herbal "magick" potions soon became the witch's trademark, and many wise old women were hanged and burned because of their "forbidden knowledge."

In today's modern world, many witches continue to use herbs for healing.

Herbal remedies are nature's cures; in some cases, safer alternatives to artificially prepared medicines with dangerous side effects. But do not ingest any herbal remedy without first consulting your healthcare provider. Some plants are highly toxic or can cause unforeseen medical problems.

Herbs grow wild in all parts of the country and are usually free for the picking, if you know what you're looking for.

Most people who do not understand wild plants tend to think of them as ugly, troublesome weeds and are happy to be rid of them. They even pay to have them "weeded" from their lawns and gardens.

If you are unable to gather your own wild-growing herbs, you should be able to buy them in most health food stores, pharmacies, herb farms and occult shops.

A fun and money-saving alternative to purchasing herbs from a store is to plant and grow your own magickal herb garden!

Good Old-Fashioned Witches' Remedies for Whatever Ails Ye
To prepare herbal teas for medicinal purposes, always use one teaspoon of herb to one cup of boiling water. Crush the leaves of fresh or dried herbs and place them in an earthenware teapot. Fill with boiling water and steep for five minutes. (Teas made from roots or seeds must be boiled for 10–15 minutes in order to extract the full flavor of the herb.) After the tea has steeped, strain it through a cheesecloth and then add honey or sugar if a sweetener is desired.

(IMPORTANT: Herbal preparations should *never* be boiled in aluminum vessels! Use only copper, earthenware or Pyrex to avoid contamination of the medicines. Please follow all directions carefully!)

ANIMAL BITES (MINOR WOUNDS)—The powdered root of angelica (gathered when the moon is in Leo, preferably) mixed with a bit of pitch and laid on the biting of dogs, or any other creature, helps to cleanse the open wound and makes it heal more quickly.

ANXIETY—A tea made from catnip, chamomile or scullcap helps to relieve anxiety and nervousness.

ARTERIOSCLEROSIS (HARDENING OF THE ARTERIES)—Combine one pint of grain alcohol with one ounce of powdered dried hawthorne berries. This tincture should be given in doses ranging from one to 15 drops. (NOTE: Although hawthorne is non-toxic, it can produce dizziness if taken in large doses.)

ASTHMA—Place the soft fuzzy leaves of the mullein plant in a teapot with hot water and inhale the steam through the spout to relieve the symptoms. Another preventative against mild attacks calls for one table-spoon of sunflower oil taken at night before going to bed. A brew of skunk cabbage, garlic, onion and honey was favored by many witches as a remedy for bronchial asthma. A very old asthma remedy used by the American Indians calls for the smoking of ground red clover blossoms. The leaves of the California gum plant combined with those of the stramonium were also smoked.

ATHLETE'S FOOT—Rub onion juice between the toes two or three times daily until the condition disappears.

BACKACHE—A tea of nettle or rosinweed is recommended for aching backs by many witches.

BEE OR HORNET STING—Wash the sting with a strong tea of juniper berries and hot water or apply a fresh poultice made of mashed garlic plant three times daily. Another old- fashioned pagan home remedy for bee stings is as follows: heat bruised plantain leaves with a match until they are wilted. Do not burn them. Squeeze out the juice and apply it to the insect bite or sting.

BURNS (MINOR)—Rub the juice from the following plants

directly on the burned area: aloe vera leaves, hound's tongue leaves, plantain leaves, houseleeks or quince seeds. To make a healing herbal salve, mix together in a large enamel baking pot one lb. of lard, four ounces of beeswax and one ounce of any of the following herbs: all-heal, fleabane, Irish moss or lady's bedstraw. (Fresh, finely cut-up herbs are the best to use, but dried herbs may also be used if fresh ones cannot be obtained.) Heat the mixture in a 200 degree oven for 3½ to four hours and then strain through a cheesecloth into a clean, heat-proof container. Allow the salve to cool to room temperature before applying to the burn.

COLDS—An ancient gypsy cold remedy recommends the drinking of a syrup made from one ounce of fresh, chopped horseradish root, one pint of boiling water and honey. Another cold remedy is blessed thistle or elder flowers brewed as a tea with a bit of honey or sugar as a sweetener.

COLDS AND FEVER—To break colds and fevers, pour one pint of boiling water over one ounce of yarrow. Add one teaspoon of honey and three drops of Tabasco sauce. Let stand approximately 10 minutes, and drink while still warm. This old witches' remedy will open up the pores and cause profuse sweating to purify the blood of toxins.

CONSTIPATION—A strong tea made from powdered licorice root and castor oil will produce a powerful laxative effect. Other herbal teas recommended include: bunchberry, horehound and red mulberry.

COUGHS—*Witches' Syrup #1*: Cover three-quarter ounce of fresh Coltsfoot leaves and one-quarter ounce of Irish moss with one pint of water and boil down until only one cup remains. Strain and add honey, bringing the syrup to a boil. Remove from heat, let the syrup cool and then bottle it. Take as needed in tablespoon doses.

Witches' Syrup #2: Boil down two or three ounces of sunflower seeds in one quart of water. Add a bit of gin and honey and take three times daily.

DANDRUFF—Steep one ounce of rosemary in a pint of boiling water. Cool and then massage into the scalp after washing and rinsing the hair.

DEPRESSION—Meditation with saffron tea is recommended.

DIARRHEA—Put one ounce of St. John's wort into a pint of boiling blackberry brandy. Cool and then take in wineglass doses. The following herb teas are also recommended: crowfoot, peppermint, red raspberry and slippery elm.

ECZEMA AND PSORIASIS—Brew a strong potion of powdered Goldenseal root, comfrey root, witch hazel bark, white oak bark and pure mountain spring water. Allow potion to cool, then soak a clean white cloth in it and apply it directly to the skin. (For external use only.)

EYE AILMENTS—Put one ounce of eyebright herb in a pint of boiling water. After it has cooled, bathe the eyes with the infusion.

FATIGUE—According to a 16th century prescription: "Seethe much rosemary herbe and bathe therein to make thee lusty, lively, joyfull, likeing and youngly."

FEVER—Boil two tablespoons of cayenne pepper in one cup of water. Cool and then add two tablespoons of sugar or honey and a bit of orange juice. Drink often until the fever subsides. Lemon balm tea is also highly recommended to reduce fever: Pour one pint of boiling water over one ounce of lemon balm. Infuse for 15–20 minutes, cool, strain and then drink. Honey, lemon peel or sugar may be added to sweeten the flavor, if desired.

GOUT—Brew a tea from strawberry leaves and flowers of the broom plant. Add cherry juice to sweeten and drink often.

GUM IRRITATION—Add one-half teaspoon of myrrh to one-third glass of lukewarm water and use as a mouthwash. Repeat as often as needed.

HALITOSIS (BAD BREATH)—Place one-third teaspoon each of rosemary, anise, and mint in a cup of boiling water. Steep for ten minutes and then strain. After cooling use as a mouthwash.

HEADACHE—Peppermint, rosemary, catnip and sage teas are excellent for treating the pain of headaches. Tea brewed from the bark of the willow tree is another effective headache remedy. Willow tree bark contains salicin, a substance which changes in the human system to salicylic acid—the active ingredient of common aspirin.

IMPOTENCY—Brew a tea from ginseng root and juniper berries and drink it when the moon is in Scorpio to help stimulate the sex organs and increase sexual drive.

INSOMNIA—Add one-quarter teaspoon of valerian root, one-quarter teaspoon of skullcap, and one-quarter teaspoon of lady's slipper to one cup of boiling water. (Never boil valerian root!) Add some honey or sugar to sweeten the tea and allow it to cool before drinking. (Do not drink more than one cup per day.) Other herbs valued for overcoming insomnia are teas of basil, catnip, chamomile, hops, lemon verbena, passionflower and violet leaves.

KIDNEY STONES—Add one ounce of trailing arbutus leaves to one pint of boiling water. Drink this several times daily.

MENOPAUSE—Brew a tea from the life root (also known as the female regulator) and squaw weed. Drink once a day before going to bed.

MENSTRUAL PAIN—Boil squaw weed and motherwort herb in a pot of water. Let it cool. Add a bit of brandy and then let it stand for a few days before drinking. The following herb teas are also recommended for men-strual cramps and discomfort: catnip, chamomile, ginger, pennyroyal and sweet cicely.

MUSCLE ACHES AND PAINS—Boil arborvitae leaves in lard to make a healing herbal salve. Apply externally to the painful area.

POISON IVY—Rub the infected area with the juice of jimson-weed. Use externally only! Jimsonweed is poisonous when taken internally.

RHEUMATISM—Pound two cloves of garlic with honey and take for three consecutive nights. (NOTE: The garlic plant was worshipped for many centuries by the gypsies for its remarkable medicinal powers and for its unique ability to scare away vampires!)

RINGWORMS—Mix one ounce of powdered bloodroot root and three ounces of lard. Bring the mixture to a boil, simmer for a short period of time and then strain. Apply this ointment to the affected area. (For external use only.)

SORE FEET—Make a soothing foot bath by brewing a strong tea of fresh alder leaves and soak the feet in it. The fresh leaves of the alder when applied directly to the bare feet also offer excellent relief for burning and soreness.

SORE THROAT—Mix one ounce of dried agrimony with one pint of boiling water. Sweeten with honey and drink warm. Another old sore throat remedy is as follows: Boil one-half ounce of bruised sassafras root, one ounce of anise seeds and two ounces of honey in one quart of water for 25–30 minutes and then add one-half pint of spirits of wine. Take as often as needed. In addition to herbal syrups, many witches recommend gargling with sage tea to soothe minor sore throat irritation.

SPLINTERS—Fill a widemouthed bottle with a mixture of aloe vera, sea salt and boiling water. Place the injured

area over the mouth of the bottle and push down
tightly. The heat and pressure should draw out the
splinter or loosen it for easy removal.

TOOTHACHE—Rub oil of cloves or juice of angelica directly
on the toothache to help numb the pain. The herbs of
grindelia, raw cow parsnip, sweet cicely and yarrow
also reduce toothache pain when placed directly into
a cavity. For baby's teething pain, a tea made of hops
is quite effective.

ULCERS OF THE STOMACH—Simmer the fresh root of the dog-
tooth violet or the adder's tongue in milk and drink.

UPSET STOMACH—Make a sauce by beating sorrel leaves
into a mash and adding a bit of sugar and vinegar.
Drink to help relieve stomach pain and gas. A broth
made from rosemary and the leaves of the western
gun plant also offers good relief from an upset stomach or indigestion. The following herbal teas are also
highly recommended: chamomile, marigold leaves,
mint, peppermint, slippery elm, valerian and yarrow.

WARTS—Rub the warts with milkweed juice three times
daily until they disappear.

Glossary of Terms Used in Herbalism

ALTERATIVES—Botanicals which tend to alter a condition
and restore normal health. Alternatives are frequently
combined with aromatics, bitter tonics and
demulcents: agrimony, American mandrake,
American spikenard, bittersweet, black cohosh root,
bloodroot, blue flag root, blue nettle root, dock, horseheal root, mayapple, pipsissewa, scabwort root &
speedwell.

ANTI-ASTHMATICS—Botanicals that are smoked or taken internally to relieve bronchial asthma: California gum
plant leaves, daisy, nettle, red clover ground blossoms
and yerba santa.

ANTISEPTICS—Botanicals which destroy the microorganisms responsible for causing infection: blue gentian extract, costmary, dead nettle, dogwood bark, Egyptian onion, elder, eucalyptus leaves and oil, garlic, horseheal root, horseradish, indigo broom, oak bark, plantain, scabwort root, smooth sumac bark, violet and witch hazel.

ANTISPASMODICS—Botanicals which prevent or relieve involuntary muscle spasms and cramps such as charley horses, epilepsy and menstrual pain: blue cohosh, cajeput, passion vine and roman chamomile.

APHRODISIACS—Plants that stimulate the sex organs and intensify sexual desire: elder, ginger, ginseng, hazel, jasmine, juniper, lavender, lemon verbena, lovage, mandrake root, serpentaria root and sundew.

AROMATICS—Fragrant herbs used in potpourris, sachets, oils, scented candles, perfumes, etc.: acacia flowers, angelica root, anise seed, bugle, burdock, calamus root, caraway, cardamon seeds, cinnamon, clove, coriander, honeysuckle, lavender, lemon verbena, lilac blossoms, mace, mint leaves, nutmeg, orange blossoms and leaves, orris root, rosemary, rose petals, southernwood, St. John's wort, sweet peak, violet, wintergreen.

ASTRINGENTS—Botanicals which cause contraction of the skin tissues: agrimony, alder bark, alum root, avens, bayberry bark and roots, bearberry leaves, black alder bark, blackberry root, black birch leaves, black cohosh, bugle, costmary, dead nettle, dock, dogwood bark, eucalyptus oil, European birch bark, fluxweed, goldenrod, hawthorne berries, hepatica, holly berries and leaves, horseheal root, Jacob's ladder, manzanita leaves and fruits, oak bark, periwinkle, pipsissewa, potentilla, scabwort root, shepherd's purse, smooth sumac seed heads, southernwood, St. John's wort, sweet fern, trailing arbutus, wax myrtle, white birch bark, wintergreen, witch hazel and yarrow.

BITTER TONICS—Botanicals with a bitter taste which stimulate the flow of gastric juices and saliva, increase the appetite and aid digestion: black haw bark, blessed thistle, bugle, dandelion, dogwood, goldenseal root and wild cherry bark.

CATHARTICS—Botanicals and other substances which cause evacuation of the bowels. Cathartics are divided into two categories: laxatives and purgatives. A laxative produces gentle bowel stimulation while purgatives induce more forceful evacuation to relieve severe constipation. *Laxatives*: aloe vera, balmony, boneset, bunchberry, chickory, dandelion, dock, horehound, horseradish, hydrangea, magnolia, olive oil, red mulberry fruit, walnuts, white ash bark. *Purgatives*: barberry, blue flag, castor oil, chaparral tea (or spurge), fennel, mayapple, poinciana leaves and senna leaves.

DEMULCENTS—Substances taken internally which soften and smooth inflamed mucous membranes and are used to treat coughs and minor throat irritations: blessed thistle, borage, coltsfoot, goldenseal root, hound's tongue and Solomon's seal.

DIAPHORETICS—Substances taken internally to increase sweating. Such substances are also called sudorifics and are frequently used to break common colds and fevers, and to promote good health: black cohosh, broom, cajeput, calendula, catnip, chamomile, elder flowers, garlic, ginger root, horseheal, hyssop, Jacob's ladder, linden flowers, mugwort, oregano, pennyroyal, rosebay, saffron, salad burnet, scabwort, serpentaria root, vervain and yarrow.

DIURETICS—Plants which increase urine secretion and work to correct urinary disorders: agrimony, balm, bearberry, black cohosh, blue cohosh, blue flag, boneset, broom, chicory, cleavers, cucumber seeds, daphne bark and root, garlic, germander, gravel root, ground cedar, horseheal, horseradish, horsetails, hydrangea,

joe-pye weed, juniper berries, parsley, pipsissewa,
pumpkin seeds, rosebay, rue, scabwort, shepherd's
purse, sorrel, sunflower seeds, vervain, wild carrot,
wood sage, wormwood and yarrow.

EMETICS—Plants which induce vomiting: adder's tongue,
bay, black mustard seeds, blue flag, bloodroot,
cliffrose, elkweed roots, hedge- hyssop, ilex berries,
mandrake, mayapple, wake-robin roots and white
mustard seeds.

EXPECTORANTS—Botanicals which loosen phlegm of the mucous membranes and promote its expulsion: benzoin,
bloodroot, chokecherry, coltsfoot, garlic, horehound
leaves, licorice root, slippery elm bark, storax tree bark
gum, sunflower seeds, sweet gum, vervain, violet,
white pine dried inner bark and yerba santa leaves.

SEDATIVES—Herbs which sooth, calm nervousness and
tranquilize: bugleweed, catnip, chamomile leaves,
fennel, Heal-All, hop vine oil, horsebalm, linden
flowers, New Jersey tea, passion vine, scullcap, skunk
cabbage root, valerian, viburnum and witch hazel.

STIMULANTS—Herbs which increase or speed up the various functional actions of the human body: angelica,
bayberry bark and roots, black pepper, bloodroot,
calendula, caraway, cayenne pepper, coriander, elder
flowers, garlic, horseheal root, horseradish, lavender,
mayweed, nettle, nutmeg, pennyroyal, pine, prickly
ash bark, rosebay, sassafras root, scabwort root,
serpentaria root, sweet flag, vervain, wild ginger,
wintergreen, wormwood and yarrow.

STOMACHIC—Plants which have curative properties in
easing disorders of the stomach: angelica, avens,
blessed thistle, blue gentian, bogbean, burdock leaves,
cayenne, elecampane, ginseng, gum plant, hop plant,
lemon verbena, oyster plant, peppermint, roman
chamomile, rosemary, salsify, spearmint, sweet flag
and yerba buena.

TONICS—Plants which strengthen or invigorate the body and stimulate general health: agrimony, avens, barberries, bayberry bark and roots, bloodroot, burdock, chamomile, chickory, coltsfoot, dandelion, ginger, goldenrod, horehound, joe-pye weed, mint, pipsissewa, red clover, rue, sea holly, selfheal, speedwell, sweet fern, sweet flag, tansy, vervain, watercress, witch hazel, wood sage, wormwood and yarrow.

VULNERARY—Herbs which are used to treat minor external wounds such as burns, cuts and scrapes: allheal, comfrey, horsetail grass, marshmallow root and plantain.

Dangerous Plants

Avoid using or experimenting with the plants that are listed in this section. Some of them possess highly potent medical properties and should only be used by experienced professional herbalists. Many of the botanicals included in the following list of dangerous plants are poisonous in part or in whole and can cause serious illness or death if not used properly.

Aconite
Arnica
Baneberry
Belladonna
Bittersweet
Black nightshade
Blue flag
Burning bush
Calabar bean
Calico bush
Camphor
Castor oil plant (seeds)
Celandine
Christmas rose (root)
Cowbane
Daffodils
Deadly nightshade
Dog's mercury (seeds)
Elkweed
Ergot
Fava bean
Flag lily
Foxglove
Gelsemium
Hellebore
Hemlock
Hemp

Henbane
Holly (seeds)
Honeysuckle (vine and fruits)
Horse balm
Ilex
Impatiens pallida
Indian arrowroot
Indian hemp
Indian tobacco
Inkberry
Jack-in-the-pulpit (root)
Jerusalem cherry
Jimsonweed
Laburnum (seeds)
Laurel (seeds)
Lily of the valley (seeds)
Lobelia
Mandrake
Mayapple (root, leaves, seeds)
Mayflower
Milkweed
Mistletoe (seeds)
Monkshood
Mountain laurel
Nux vomica
Oleander
Ordeal bean
Opium poppy
Pigeonberry
Poinsetta (leaves)
Poison dogwood
Poison flag
Poison hemlock
Poison ivy
Poison oak

Poison sumac
Poke
Pokeberry
Poke root
Pokeweed
Rhubarb leaves
Rosebay
Snow on the mountain
Spingle tree (seeds)
Spotted hemlock
Spurge
Stramonium
Swallow wort
Thorn apple
Tobacco
Wahoo
Wake-robin
Water dropwort
Water hemlock
White bryony
White hellebore
White snakeroot
Winter rose
Wolfsbane
Wood anemone (seeds)
Wormwood
Yellow jasmine
Yew (seeds and berries)

5

Spellcasting

Note

WHEN WORKING THE SPELLS that follow, it is important to observe all instructions carefully. Herbs are extremely powerful and each possesses its own magickal property. Therefore, in order to work a spell properly and achieve the right results, it is imperative that no herbal substitutions or omissions be attempted.

Most herbs can be bought in local occult shops (if you are lucky enough to have one), herb farms, and occasionally health food stores and pharmacies. But often the more esoteric herbs such as mandrake root or mugwort can be difficult to obtain. This is the reason that many witches prefer to buy their herbs from mail-order herb suppliers.

Buying herbs through the mail offers several advantages. Many of the mail-order herb companies are run by witches or other people who understand the craft and therefore carry a more complete selection of magickal herbs than the corner pharmacy or health food store. There are also many witches (especially those who live in small towns or areas where witchcraft is not accepted) who prefer ordering herbs and other occult supplies through the mail in order to protect their privacy and prevent their identity as a witch from becoming public knowledge.

The following is a list of mail order herb dealers who specialize in hard to find magickal herbs. (Please note: Certain exotic and poisonous magickal herbs such as hemlock and belladonna unfortunately have been made illegal and the only way to obtain them is to go out into the wild and gather your own.) This list has been made as up to date as possible. Some of these companies will mail out free catalogues upon request, others charge a few dollars and some charge but will refund your money after an order has been placed. Since all prices are subject to change, it is advisable to write or call for current catalogue prices.

13 MOONS
497 Main Street
Bennington, VT 05201
(802) 681-7082
info@13moons.com
www.13moons.com

PENN HERB COMPANY
601 North 2nd Street
Philadelphia, PA 19123
(215) 632-6100
www.pennherb.com

ARTES AND CRAFT
(269) 621-2221
artesncraft@gmail.com
artesandcraft.com

STARWEST BOTANICALS
161 Main Avenue
Sacramento, CA 95838
(800) 800-4372
www.starwest-botanicals.com

ALCHEMY WORKS
P.O. Box 14098
East Providence, RI 02914
(607) 737-9250
www.alchemy-works.com
admin@alchemy-works.com

ENCHANTMENTS
424 East 9th Street New York, NY 10009
(212) 228-4394
www.enchantmentsincnyc.com

THE CROOKED PATH
2020 W. Magnolia Blvd.
Burbank, CA 91506
(818) 736-5919
www.thecrookedpathshop.com

TAO OF HERBS, INC.
240 W. 31st Street
Chicago, IL 60616
(312) 881-0078
(888) 828-8228
www.taoofherbs.com
info@taoofherbs.com
help@taoofherbs.com

ARCANA HERBAL
2834 W 44th Avenue
Denver, CO 80211
(720) 389-7214
Hello@ArcanaHerbal.com
www.arcanaherbal.com
www.etsy.com/shop/arcanaherbalco

SHAMAN'S GARDEN
Motueka
Tasman, 7120
New Zealand
shaman.co.nz

HARMONIC ARTS
2660 Dunsmuir Ave.
P.O. Box 659
Cumberland, British Columbia
V0R 1S0
Canada
(844) 871-4054
help@harmonicarts.ca
harmonicarts.ca

CATSKILL MOUNTAIN HERBALS
P.O. Box 1426
Olivebridge, NY 12461
(845)-657-2943
wfeather108@gmail.com
www.catskillmountainherbals.com

HERB PHARM
20260 Williams Highway
Williams, OR 97544
(541) 846-6262
www.herb-pharm.com

Amulets and Talismans

Amulets and talismans are powerful magickal objects that are used to protect against evil influences, counteract illness and attract good luck.

There are some people who think that an amulet and a talisman are the same thing, and although they work in similar ways, there is a big difference between the two. Amulets are nature-made while talismans are objects created by human hands.

COWRIE SHELL AMULET—Wear a cowrie shell to increase sexualpotency or place the shell on a grave to ensure the immortality of the dead buried below.

MANDRAKE AMULET—Wear a mandrake root to cure ill health and to protect against influences of evil.

TURQUOISE AMULET—Wear an amulet made of turquoise to protect against the power of the evil eye and other influences of evil and sorcery.

ANTI-SORCERY AMULETS—Suspend a red onion from the ceiling or a bedpost to protect against sorcery and keep away influences of evil. Wear a necklace of chicken bones around your neck to protect against black magick and psychic attacks. A black stone with a hole keeps away evil and works as a powerful jinx-breaker.

ANTI-NIGHTMARE AMULET—Hang a small wreath of gray feathers over a bed to prevent nightmares and bring restful sleep.

PENTAGRAM TALISMAN—Inscribe the powerful magickal symbol of a pentagram on a lodestone or a triangular piece of copper and carry it in your pocket for good health.

PROTECTION TALISMAN—On a square piece of paper or parchment, write the ancient magickal formula:

S A T O R
A R E P O
T E N E T
O P E R A
R O T A S

GARLIC—Garlic worn around the neck keeps away evil forces, especially vampires!

GOOD LUCK AMULETS AND TALISMANS—The most common good luck amulets are four-leaf clovers and the rabbit's foot. The most common good luck talismans are birthstone rings, horseshoes and pennies. A blue string with seven knots will help to protect against evil and bring good luck to a house. To attract good fortune wear an amulet of sarsaparilla root around your neck, light a green candle and chant thrice: "BAD LUCK DECLINE; GOOD LUCK BE MINE."

PYRAMID TALISMAN—Pyramid-shaped crystals bring wisdom and balance the emotional qualities. When placed under a bed, they protect the sleeper from psychic attack by others.

GOLD COIN TALISMAN—Wear a gold coin on a chain around your neck to attract success and wealth.

UNICORN TALISMAN—Unicorn-shaped jewelry will protect the wearer from all enemies when the magickal words "NOCTAR" and "RAIBAN" are recited three times.

Aphrodisiacs

MANDRAKE APHRODISIAC—To create a powerful aphrodisiac, add a *tiny* particle of powdered female mandrake leaf to a cup of wine. (Use caution when working with mandrake root, both male and female, for it is a very magickal plant and misuse of it can result in delirium or painful death.)

APHRODISIAC SACHET—During a full moon, place an herb mixture of verbana, lemon, serpentaria root and elder flowers on the center of a square of red felt or cotton. Gather up the ends and tie them together with red wool yarn or cotton twine. Place this powerful sachet under your pillow or wear it on a string around your neck.

VENUS APHRODISIA WINE—Boil two teaspoons of passion fruit juice, two powdered juniper berries and a pinch of ground dried basil in red wine while chanting:

VENUS WINE BUBBLE AND TURN
PASSION BURN
PASSION BURN

LOVE POTION TEA

1 pinch rosemary
2 teaspoons black tea
3 pinches thyme
3 pinches nutmeg
3 fresh mint leaves
6 fresh rose petals
6 lemon leaves

To make another person fall in love with you, brew this tea on a Friday during a waxing moon.

Place all ingredients in an earthenware or copper tea kettle. Boil three cups of pure spring water and add to the kettle. Sweeten with sugar or honey, if desired.

Before drinking, recite this magickal rhyme:

BY LIGHT OF MOON WAXING I BREW THIS
  TEA
TO MAKE (name) DESIRE ME.

Drink some of the tea and then say:

GODDESS OF LOVE HEAR NOW MY PLEA LET
  [name] DESIRE ME!

SO MOTE IT BE SO MOTE IT BE

On the following Friday, brew another pot of the love potion tea and give some to the person you want to love you. He or she will soon begin to fall in love with you.

Yarrow Love-Vision Spell

To receive a psychic dream vision of your future lover, sew an ounce of yarrow herb into a small square of red flannel and place it under your pillow at bedtime. Close your eyes and recite these magickal words:

THOU HERBE OF VENUS TREE THY TRUE
  NAME IS YARROW;
NOW WHO MY TRUE LOVE MUST BE PRAY
TELL THOU ME TOMORROW.

Three Spells to Make a Lover Return

SPELL 1—Prick the ring finger of your left hand with a pin
of silver, and with the blood, write both your name
and the name of your lover on a round piece of white
silk. With ashes of burnt basil (the herb of love), draw
one circle surrounding both names on the silk. Fold
the cloth in half and then fold over again. Stick the
silver pin through the folded silk to hold it and then
bury it in the earth at midnight on the third night of
the waxing moon.

SPELL 2—Nail a branch of hazel over your door and leave
it there for two weeks to make your lover return to
you.

SPELL 3—For maximum effectiveness, the following spell
should be performed on a Friday when the moon is
either in Taurus or Libra. (Venus, the planet of love, is
the ruler over these two signs. It is also the ruling
planet of the sixth day of the week.) Stick a needle
through the wick of a RED candle. Light the candle
and concentrate on your lover as you recite this
incantation:

LIGHT OF VENUS, LIGHT OF LOVE;
BURN IN (lover's name) HEART
AND RETURN HIS/HER LOVE TO ME.

Poppets

A poppet is a cloth doll, similar to a voodoo doll, but used in white magick spells for love and healing.

To make a poppet, you will need two pieces of cloth equal in size, scissors, needle, thread, ink or paint and herbs to stuff the doll.

Concentrating on the man or woman the poppet will represent, draw the outline of the person on one of the pieces of cloth. Place it over the other piece of cloth and then carefully cut along the outline with scissors to make two identical doll patterns. With a needle and thread, sew together the two pieces of cloth along the seams but leave the seam at the top of the head open for stuffing.

The next step is to draw the person's facial features, characteristics (such as moustache, beard, glasses, hair, etc.) and his or her astrological symbol on the torso of the poppet with ink or paint.

If the poppet is made to be used in a love spell, it should be stuffed with mugwort, feverfew, sorrel or any other herb ruled by Venus, the planet of love. If a spell involving healing is to be performed, the poppet should be stuffed with the herbs that are healing to the person's ailment. (See Chapter 4, "Herbs" for further information on their healing properties.)

After the poppet has been stuffed, the opening at the top of its head should be sewn shut to prevent the herbs from falling out.

The poppet is now ready to be used. When the moon is waxing, lay the poppet in the center of the altar and sprinkle it with salted water to consecrate it. As you do this, say:

WITH THIS SALT AND WATER I CONSECRATE
  THEE

Pick up your athame with your left hand. Touch the poppet with the athame to charge it with magickal power and say:

I CHARGE THEE
BY THE DIVINE POWERS
OF THE GOD AND GODDESS

Incense and candles should now be lit. (Red candles for love spells and white candles for healing.)

Pick up the poppet and hold it in your hands. Concentrate on the love or healing of the person whom the poppet represents and direct your power into it. Recite the person's name nine times, shouting it loudly on the ninth recitation.

Return the poppet to the center of the altar and tie a red ribbon (representing love) or a white ribbon (representing healing) around its body. Place the athame on top of it and leave on the center of the altar for three weeks.

After completing the ritual, wrap the poppet in a white satin or silk cloth, leaving the ribbon tied to it, and keep it in a safe and secret place where it will never be disturbed.

To reverse a poppet love spell, you must untie the ribbon from the poppet, remove the herbs and burn the poppet as you recite the following words:

BY THE DIVINE POWERS
IF THE GOD AND GODDESS I NOW REMOVE
    THIS SPELL
LET [name] LOVE ME NO MORE

Mix the ashes with the herbs and bury the mixture in the ground during a waning moon.

In the event that the person represented by the poppet should pass away, the poppet should be wrapped in a black cloth and buried along with the person, if possible. If this cannot be done, then burn the poppet and bury the ashes under the shadow of an oak tree.

Ritual to Improve Psychic Abilities

Three days before the full moon (preferably when it is in Cancer, Pisces, or Scorpio), light 13 purple-colored candles to help attract psychic influences. Gaze into a mirror, crystal ball or crystal pyramid and chant three times:

ASARIEL, ARCHANGEL OF NEPTUNE AND
  RULER OF CLAIRVOYANCE, OPEN MY
  THIRD EYE
AND SHOW ME THE HIDDEN LIGHT. LET ME
  PERCEIVE THE KINGDOMS OF THE
  UNKNOWN.
LET ME UNDERSTAND THE WISDOM OF THE
  UNIVERSE.

After chanting, relax your mind, do not permit any negative thoughts, breathe slowly and concentrate on opening your Third Eye.

The Third Eye, located in the space between the eyebrows, is the body's highest source of power.

Purification of the Soul

To purify the soul, brew a tea made from ginseng root, light a white candle and, before drinking the tea, recite the following pagan prayer to the sacred Goddess:

O GODDESS, BEAUTIFUL AND FAIR LET YOUR
   DIVINE SPIRIT FLOW INTO THIS EARTHLY
   SUBSTANCE SO THAT HE/SHE WHO
   DRINKS IT
MAY BE CLEANSED OF ALL IMPURITIES OF
   THE SOUL. SO MOTE IT BE.

As you drink the blessed Ginseng tea and feel its warmth filling your insides, the divine spirit of the Goddess will enter you and purify your soul.

+

Anti-Succubus/Incubus Spell

A succubus is a demon or evil spirit that takes on the shape of a beautiful woman and seduces sleeping males in order to possess their souls.

An incubus is the male counterpart taking the form of a handsome man and seducing sleeping females.

For protection against a succubus or incubus, it is advisable to place mugwort under your pillow at night and recite the following incantation before going to sleep:

GODDESS OF THE NIGHT WATCH OVER AND
PROTECT ME AS I SLEEP AND DREAM.

SHIELD MY SOUL FROM HARM AND SHINE
YOUR DIVINE LIGHT
TO KEEP AWAY THE SPIRITS OF EVIL.

Remedy for the Bewitched

Mix 13 drops of the bewitched person's blood with rosemary balm, marigolds, salt and ale. On a starless night, light seven new white candles and give this mixture to the bewitched person to drink. Whatever magick power or charm he or she is under will be instantly dissolved.

Spell to Acquire Wealth

On a night when the moon is in Sagittarius, wear a talisman of seven gold rings on a gold chain and light five green candles to symbolize fertility and abundance. As you place a coin under each candle, say:

SPIRITS OF GOOD FORTUNE HEAR MY VERSE.
MONEY AND SILVER FILL MY PURSE.

After placing a coin under all five candles and reciting the verse five times, close your eyes and concentrate on images of money. Continue concentrating until all five candles have burned themselves out.

In time, you will begin to acquire small or large amounts of money. Be patient. Do not expect a pot of gold to suddenly appear before your eyes.

Witchcraft works in mysterious ways.

Wart-Curing Spell

Prick each wart with a pin blackened over the flame from a white candle and place three drops of blood from each wart on an onion. Bury the onion at a crossroad when the moon is in a fire sign (Aries, Leo or Sagittarius). As the onion decays, the warts will disappear.

The Abracadabra Talisman

A very ancient and well-known magickal cure for fever or illness calls for the writing of the word "ABRA-CADABRA" on a piece of white paper 11 times, dropping a letter in each line to form an inverted pyramid:

abracadabra
abracadabr
abracadab
abracada
abracad
abraca
abrac
abra
abr
ab
a

Tie the paper around the neck with flax, wear it for nine days and nights, and then throw it backwards over your left shoulder into a stream flowing eastward.

Fever-Curing Spell

With blood from the thumb of your right hand, write on a piece of white paper:

abraxas

abraxa

abrax

abra

abr

ab

a

Place the talisman against your forehead and the power of the abraxas pyramid will help to reduce the fever.

Magic Herb Pillow

To cure insomnia, stuff a pillow with catnip, passion-flowers and hops just before bedtime. Lie down with the back of your head touching the pillow and recite the following chant three times aloud:

CATNIP, PASSIONFLOWERS, HOPS IN THIS PIL-
 LOW 'NEATH MY HEAD
BRING PEACEFUL REST TO ME AND STOP
THE SLEEPNESSNESS THAT PLAGUES MY BED

Close your eyes and think of something pleasant. Soon you will fall asleep and dream.

HERBAL SLEEP POTION

Chamomile
Fennel seed
Rosebuds
Mugwort
Peppermint
Jasmine

Put the herb mixture in a clear glass jar with pure mountain spring water.
Face the east and chant:

BLESSED BE THIS BREW IN THE NAME OF
WODEN. BLESSED BE THIS BREW NI THE
NAME OF FREYA.

Cap the jar tightly and allow it to sit in the sun for a whole day until the spring water is colored by the herbs. Strain the brew through a cheesecloth or bamboo strainer and drink before going to bed. It will help you to relax and have a pleasant night's sleep. (This is also an excellent tea to drink if you are plagued by nightmares.)

Wind-Cantation (to summon the wind)

With wand or athame held tightly in the right hand and pointing straight forward, stand facing the east and say:

COME HITHER, SPIRITS OF THE EAST WIND
I COMMAND THEE BY THE NAME YOD HE
    VAU HE ELEMENTAL KING OF AIR.

Turn to the south and say:

COME HITHER, SPIRITS OF THE SOUTH WIND
I COMMAND THEE BY THE NAME ADONAI
ELEMENTAL KING OF FIRE.

Turn to the west and say:

COME HITHER, SPIRITS OF THE WEST WIND
I COMMAND THEE BY THE NAME EHEIEH
    ELEMENTAL KING OF WATER.

Turn to the north and say:

COME HITHER, SPIRITS OF THE NORTH WIND
I COMMAND THEE BY THE NAME AGLA
    ELEMENTAL KING OF EARTH.

Witches' Curse Cakes

SPELL AND RECIPE—To bring ill health to an enemy, bake a
lock of their hair or a few of their fingernail clippings
in a curse cake and bury it under a dead tree during a
waning moon. As the cake decays, so will the enemy's
health decline.

WITCHES' CURSE CAKE

½ cup flour
¼ teaspoon powdered mandrake root
¼ teaspoon baking powder
½ teaspoon salt
1 egg
¼ cup of sour milk

Preheat oven to 450 degrees. Grease the inside of a small tin tray or one cup of a muffin tin. Combine the flour, mandrake root, baking powder, salt, egg and milk. Beat well until the batter is smooth. Add your enemy's lock of hair and/or fingernail clippings and stir well. Spoon the batter into the tin tray, filling about halfway to the top. Bake 20–25 minutes or until the curse cake is brown.

Spell for Hexing Enemies

Take a glove or other small item of clothing belonging to your enemy and boil it in a cauldron (or large pot) filled with water mixed with wilted rue leaves, chimney soot and the urine from a black cat. Stir six times. Remove the glove from the vile brew, prick it thrice with a silver pin and chant twice:

WITH SILVER PIN
I PRICK THE ONE
WHOSE NAME IS [name of enemy]
TO HIM/HER LET HARM BE DONE!

By the light of a waning moon, dig a hole and bury the glove. After covering the hole with dirt, spit twice on it, close your eyes and say:

I CURSE THEE
BY THE GREAT POWER OF ARIOCH
ENEMY BE CURSED!

To lift the curse, dig up the glove and burn it in fire. As it burns, say:

FIRE BURN, ASHES TURN.
EVIL SPIRITS DISPERSE.
I NOW REMOVE THIS CURSE.

Counterspells

To break the power of an evil witch's spell and turn the black magick back upon the instigator, an old 17th-century counterspell from Salem calls for the boiling of pins or needles in a pot filled with the urine of the bewitched victim.

In 1692, a variation on urine boiling was conducted at Salem. The counterspell called for the baking of a spell-breaking cake, made from rye meal and the victim's urine. To cure the afflicted person, the cake would be fed to the animal identified as the witch's familiar.

One of the most common countercharms used in 17th-century Salem for a bewitched animal was to cut off its ear and boil or burn it in a fire.

In the 17th century (and still today), certain herbs were used by witches and nonwitches alike to keep away evil influences, reverse spells and cure those afflicted by sorcery. Bay, dill, garlic and St. John's wort were the most effective and popular anti-sorcery herbs used.

Anti-Hex Talisman and Spells

TALISMAN—To make a powerful anti-hex talisman, engrave on a gemstone the mystical word "DAVAR." Hold the talisman to your forehead, close your eyes and say:

WORDS OF POWER BE SPOKEN;
POWER OF THE HEX BE BROKEN.

SPELL—On a piece of blue paper write the powerful magick words:

ATEH
MALKUTH VE
GEBURAH VE
GEDULAH LE
OLAHM

Burn the paper over a white candle during the time of a full moon or an eclipse, and with the ashes, rub the symbol of an "X" on your forehead to neutralize the power of the hex.

Six Evil Eye Countercharms

1 To neutralize or reverse the effects of the Evil Eye, wear a clove of garlic around your neck on a white string or carry a piece of garlic in your pocket. This is an ancient Evil Eye repellent that works quite well.

2 Another method to deal with the power of the Evil Eye calls for the burning of peacock feathers and throwing the ashes in a stream or river.

3 An effective spell to counteract the Evil Eye is to hold a talisman made from an iron key between your eyes and chant: "KAYN AYN HA'RAH, KAYN AYN HA'RAH, KAYN AYN HA'RAH"

4 Painting both of your eyelids with a dark blue or black eye makeup is a powerful precaution against the pernicious influence of an Evil Eye that dates back to ancient Egyptian times.

5 A necklace or bracelet made of blue colored beads makes an effective talisman to ward off the power of the Evil Eye.

6 A potent Latin American gesture to avert the influence of the Evil Eye is to place the thumb between the first and second fingers and then spit three times.

Protection Against Evil

3 angelica leaves
5 marjoram leaves
7 bay leaves
1 cup pure spring water

In a small pot, boil the water and leaves for one minute. Remove from heat and allow the liquid to cool. Then light a blue candle and say:

GODDESS OF LIFE GODDESS OF DEATH GODDESS OF ALL POWER THAT IS THE
UNIVERSE:
SHINE YOUR LIGHT OF WHITE UPON ME AND
SHIELD ME FROM ALL FORCES EVIL
MALEVOLENT AND BANEFUL.

Next, dip the index finger of your right hand into the liquid and with your fingertip draw a circle on your forehead. As you draw the circle, say:

O DIVINE GODDESS
OF THE MOON AND STARS; ENCOMPASS MY
BODY AND SOUL WITH YOUR CIRCLE OF
LIGHT AND GIVE TO ME PEACE
AND PROTECTION FROM HARM. SO MOTE IT
BE!

The remaining liquid should be sprinkled around your house or added to your bath water for additional protection.

Ceremonial Evocation of Spirits

Before performing this ceremony, it is traditional to fast with just water for three days. During this fasting period there should be much meditation, but absolutely under no circumstances should drugs, alcohol or tobacco be used. The body must be prepared by bathing in water to purify and remove all imperfections of the mind and psyche.

To evoke spirits, you will need a wand to exert influence on the spheres and to symbolize your will as a magician. It is best to use a wooden wand that has been fitted with a metal ring corresponding to the spheres:

SATURN: Lead
JUPITER: Tin
MARS: Iron
SUN: Gold
VENUS: Copper
MERCURY: Brass
MOON: Silver

Your ceremonial robe should be made of either white or black satin (depending upon which type of magick you are going to perform) with a matching belt. Elemental symbols and your own personal astrological symbols and/or coven insignia may be embroidered on the belt in red or gold.

Cast the magick circle beginning in the east and continuing clockwise for invocation and counter-clockwise for banishing spirits. The circle should be about nine feet in diameter. A large pentagram is then drawn inside of the circle with all five points of the star touching the circle. It is very important that the "top" of the pentagram star faces east.

If the circle and pentagram have been permanently drawn or painted on

the floor, then the circle must be re-cast by tracing it with your ceremonial sword, beginning and ending the circle in the east. The invoking pentagram must also be traced with the sword in the same manner.

A sprinkling of salt and water around the circle is then done to consecrate the magick circle which not only functions as an invisible, impenetrable barrier to shield the magician against any harmful forces that may try to interfere with the ceremony, but also becomes a container of psychic power and super strength.

As you walk around the circle sprinkling the water and the salt, say:

I CONSECRATE AND CONJURE THEE
O CIRCLE OF MAGICK, RING OF POWER
SYMBOL OF PERFECTION AND CONSTANT RE-
    NEWAL GUARDIAN AND PROTECTOR
ETERNAL AND INFINITE.

It is most important to remember that once the circle has been consecrated, it must not be broken and you should never attempt to leave its protection during the ceremony. Only after the ceremony when all spirits have been banished may the circle be uncast.

Five candles should be lit and placed around the magick circle—one on each of the five points of the pentagram. It is very important that the candles be of the proper symbolic color:

WHITE represents purity, spirituality and healing.
BLACK represents all negative forces, revenge and
    death.
RED represents sexual potency, love and good
    health.

GREEN represents fertility, good fortune and success.
BLUE represents protection, wisdom and occult
power.
PURPLE represents psychic awareness and the
higher realms of consciousness.

Incense should be burned to provide the proper at-
mosphere, attract spirits and stimulate the mental and
psychic senses.

Now you are ready to step into the center of the circle.
Stand facing east and hold the wand in your right hand if
you are invoking a positive spirit to aid you in performing white magick. If you are invoking a negative spirit to
aid you in black magick, you must hold the wand in your
left hand and hold a ceremonial sword or athame in your
right hand.

Concentrate on the particular spirit you wish to evoke
and then repeat out loud:

I CONJURE THEE, O SPIRIT OF _____
BY THE POWER OF THE SUPREME MAJESTY
AND BY THE POWER OF THE UNIVERSE.

RISETH FROM THE SHADOWS OF DARKNESS
AND MATERIALIZE BEFORE ME IN HUMAN
FORM FREE OF HELLISH DEFORMITY AND
HORROR.

COME, THEREFORE, IN THE HOLY NAMES JET-
ROS, ATHENOROS, PARACLETUS
AND BY THE NAME OF THE GOD WHO RULES
OVER THEE
AND TO WHOM YOU OWEST THINE
OBEDIENCE. APPEAR NOW BEFORE THIS
CIRCLE TO DO MY WILL!

I INVOKE AND COMMAND THEE, O SPIRIT OF
____BY THE SACRED POWER OF TETRAGRAMMA-
TON RETROGRAMMATON, PENTAGRAMMATON!

I INVOKE AND COMMAND THEE BY THE
POWER OF ALL GODS AND GODDESSES
WHO ARE ONE.

I INVOKE AND COMMAND THEE BY THE
HOLY NAMES OF ADONAI, ZEBAOTH,
AMIORAM
AND BY THE TRUE NAME OF THE ETERNAL
GOD.

DO THOU COME FORTHWITH, O SPIRIT SPEAK
UNTO ME IN CLEAR VOICE
THAT I MAY UNDERSTAND THEE
AND MANIFEST THAT WHICH I DESIRE.

After the magick work had been accomplished and a
thanksgiving properly expressed, you must release the
spirit from your power before closing the magick circle.
To do this, say:

O SPIRIT OF ____
THOU HAD SERVED ME WELL.
I HEREBY GRANT THEE FREEDOM TO DEPART
AND RETURN TO THY DWELLING PLACE
IN THE SHADOWS. DEPART NOW IN PEACE
AND BE THOU WILLING AND READY TO
COME WHENEVER EXORCIZED AND CON-
JURED
BY THE SACRED RITES OF MAGICK. SO MOTE
IT BE.

Uncast the magick circle by tracing it with the ceremonial sword, starting in the east and moving in a counter-

clockwise direction around the circle and ending in the east. The same tracing gesture must be done over the pentagram. Start at the top point facing east and move the sword in the reverse direction from which the pentagram was drawn until the entire star has been traced backwards.

Reconstruct the temple by removing the ritual tools from the circle and returning them to their normal storage area. Remove the ceremonial robe and belt, and like all other ritual objects, keep them in a safe undisturbed place.

No one other than the magician or coven must ever be allowed to see or touch them. And it is important that they never be used for any purpose other than working magick.

Exorcism

To perform an exorcism ritual for casting out evil spirits or demons from a person, you will need to gather together 12 white altar candles, salt, holy water and a special exorcism ointment for annointing the head and body of the possessed.

To make the exorcism ointment, add three tablespoons of frankincense oil, three tablespoons of myrrh oil, six drops of clove oil and one-half teaspoon of powdered garlic to one-quarter cup of melted animal fat. Let it cool before using.

Begin the exorcism ritual by lighting the candles and placing them around the body of the possessed man or woman. It is most important that all 12 candles remain lit throughout the entire ritual. If any should happen to go out, relight them immediately!

An incense made from Solomon's seal, Saint John's wort or angelica may also be burned during the exorcism.

Since most exorcisms can stir up violent reactions, it is advisable to perform the ritual with the possessed person lying in a supine position with arms and legs strapped down. (The straps must be secure, but not too tight as to cut off circulation.) This precautionary measure is for the possessed's own protection as well as yours.

The next step is to sprinkle some salt over the possessed person and say:

WITH THIS HOLY SALT I BAPTIZE THEE

Now sprinkle some of the holy water across the body, making the mystical sign of the "X" and say:

WITH THIS HOLY WATER I SANCTIFY THEE

The next and final step is to annoint the person's feet, stomach, palms of the hands and temples with the exorcism ointment while reciting loudly the following exorcism prayer:

HEAR ME, O DEMONIC SPIRIT
WHO POSSESSES THIS MORTAL BODY
I COMMAND THEE TO DEPART AT ONCE AND
    RETURN INTO THIS PERSON NO MORE! BY
    THE HOLY AND MIGHTY POWER
OF THE EVERLASTING SUPREME BEING I CAST
    THEE OUT!
DEPART FROM THIS MORTAL BODY AT ONCE
    THE GODS COMMAND THEE!

This powerful exorcism ritual may have to be repeated several times before any positive results are achieved.

6

Lexicon of Witchcraft

A

ABRACADABRA: a cabalistic word derived from the name
Abraxas, a mighty Gnostic deity whose name means
"hurt me not." The word abracadabra is said to
possess the magickal power to ward off illness and
to cure fever when its letters are arranged in an
inverted pyramid (a holy figure and symbol of trinity)
and worn around the neck as a talisman.

ABRAMELIN MAGICK: a semi-Gnostic form of magick that
depends heavily on word-magick and palindromic
magick squares.

AEROMANCY: divination from the sky and the air, extend-
ing beyond the range of weather prognostications
and concentrating more upon spectral formations,
shapes of clouds, comets and other phenomena of the
heavens.

AIR: one of the four elemental signs.

AIR SIGNS: the astrological signs attributed to the element of air are Aquarius, Gemini and Libra.

ALCHEMIST: one who practices the occult science of alchemy.

ALCHEMY: the ancient occult science of transmutation of base metals into gold by both chemical and spiritual processes.

ALECTRYOMANCY: divination whereby a bird, usually a black hen, is allowed to pick up grains of corn from a circle of letters to form names or words containing prophetic significance.

AMULET: a consecrated nature-made object (usually a small stone, gem or piece of metal inscribed with runes or magickal symbols) that possesses the power to protect a person or thing from threatening evil influences and to attract good luck. A four-leaf clover and a rabbit's foot are two examples of popular amulets.

ANIMISM: the spiritual belief that every thing in nature, animate as well as inanimate, possesses an innate soul as well as a body.

APPARITION: the appearance of the phantom of a person, living or dead, seen in a dream or in the waking state.

ASTRAL BODY: the double of the physical body, but made of a much finer substance with a shining and luminous appearance. The astral body is connected to the physical body by an elastic umbilical-like cord and is able to pass through solid obstructions and float about unhindered by gravity, space or time.

ASTRAL PLANE: the third plane of existence on which life takes place.

ASTRAL PROJECTION: an out-of-body experience; the separation of the consciousness from the physical body.

ASTROLOGY: an ancient occult art and science, dating back to the Third Century B.C., that judges the influence of the planets in the solar system upon the course of human affairs. In astrology, a planet's influence varies according to which section of the zodiac it is in.

ATHAME: a knife used by witches to draw the magick circle and to store and direct energy. A witch's athame has either a black or white handle (depending on the type of magick practiced) and various magickal symbols inscribed on its blade. (also spelled ARTHAME)

AUGUR: a sign or omen. Also a person who interprets the omens of birds.

AURA: a colored light produced by heat energy and electromagnetic energy that emanates from the bodies of all living things.

AUTOMATIC WRITING: a method of spirit communication by which a medium enters a dreamlike state and allows a spirit guide to control his or her hand to write messages.

AXIOMANCY: divination by an ax or hatchet. When properly interpreted, the quivers of the ax when driven into a post are said to reveal answers to questions. The way in which the ax handle falls to the ground is an old method used to point out the direction taken by a thief.

B

BANISH: to release and drive away a conjured spirit from the power of the magick circle.

BANSHEE: in Gaelic lore, a female spirit who presages a death in the family by wailing a mournful tune that sounds like the melancholy moaning of the wind. As a herald of death, the banshee is usually heard at night under the window of the person who is about to die.

BESOM: a straw broom used by witches in certain Wiccan ceremonies such as Handfasting and Candlemas. Although the broom has always been associated with witches, it was never actually used for flying. Witches practicing sympathetic magick would straddle the besom and jump up and down in order to show the crops how high to grow.

BIGGHES: a set of ceremonial jewelry consisting of a leather garter, silver crown with crescent moon, bracelet and necklace worn by a Witch Queen or a High Priestess of a coven.

BLACK ARTS: the practice of black magick.

BLACK MAGIC: the form that signifies the destructive element, devoted to causing injury or death to others.

BOKOR: a sorcerer who practices voodoo black magick.

BOOK OF SHADOWS: a secret diary of magick spells and potions kept by a witch. It is a Wiccan tradition that a witch's Book of Shadows be burned in the event of his or her death in order to protect the secrets of the craft.

BURIN: an engraving tool used by witches to mark names or symbols ritually on athames, swords, bells and other magickal tools.

C

CANDLE MAGICK: a form of sympathetic magick that uses colored candles to represent the people and things at which its spells are directed. The color of the candle is very important as each color symbolizes a different attribute, influence and emotion, as there are different astral colors for each of the 12 zodiac signs.

CELTIC CROSS: a tarot card reading method.

CENSER: an incense burner used in magick rituals.

CEREMONIAL MAGICK: the art and practice of summoning and commanding spirits through words of power.

CHAKRA: one of the seven special points of psychic energy located within the human body that begin at the genital region and end at the top of the skull.

CHARM: a highly magickal object that not only works like an amulet or talisman to counteract misfortune, but also can be used to bewitch others.

CHEIROGNOMY: the study of the shapes of hands and fingers and what they reveal about an individual's personality and physical health.

CHEIROMANCY: (PALMISTRY, PALM-READING)—the study of the lines of the palm to disclose an individual's past and to predict his or her future. There are seven important lines on the palm of the hand and seven lesser lines. The important (or main) lines are: the line of life, the line of head, the line of heart, the girdle of Venus, the line of health, the sun line and the line of destiny. The seven lesser lines are: the line of Mars, the Via Lasciva, the line of intuition, the marriage line and the three bracelet lines on the wrist.

CINGULUM: a consecrated cord, red and nine feet long used

by witches when dancing to raise power. Nine knots on the cord are used for storing built up power for future magickal use. To release the power, the knots must be untied in the exact order in which they were tied.

CLAIRAUDIENCE: an auditory form of E.S.P.

CLAIRVOYANCE: the extrasensory power to perceive objects or events that are out of the range of average human senses.

CLAIRVOYANT: a person gifted with the power of clairvoyance.

CONE OF POWER: power from a coven of witches or a solitary witch that generates and collects in the form of a cone.

CONSECRATION: the art, process or ceremony of making something sacred.

CONTACT TELEPATHY: the ability to read another person's mind through physical contact and intense concentration.

CONTROL: a spirit who speaks through a medium in trance, usually on a regular basis, and acts as an intermediary with other spirits who wish to communicate with the living.

COUNTERCHARM: a powerful magickal charm that is used to neutralize or reverse the effects of another charm or spell.

COUNTERSPELL: a powerful magickal spell that neutralizes or reverses the effects of another spell or charm.

COVEN: a group of witches led by a priest and a priestess.

COVENER: a witch, male or female, who is a member of a coven.

COVENSTEAD: the place where a coven meets.

COWAN: among witches, a person who is not a witch.

CURSE: a deliberate concentration of destructive negative energy aimed at a person, thing or place

D

DACTYLOMANCY: an early form of radiesthesia with a dangling ring indicating numbers and/or words by its swinging motion.

DEMIGOD: the semidivine offspring of a mortal and a deity.

DEMONIC POSSESSION: a condition whereby a person's physical body is invaded and taken over by evil spirits or demons who cause the sufferer to behave strangely.

DIANIC: a type of coven that worships only the Goddess or accords the Horned God secondary status to the Goddess. Dianic feminist Wicca encourages female leadership and involves its practitioners in feminist issues. Although some covens of the Dianic tradition include both female and male members, most exclude men and some are explicitly lesbian.

DIRECT WRITING: messages written by spirits without the agency of mediums or other living persons.

DIVINATION: the esoteric science, art and practice of foretelling future events. Throughout the years, different religions and cultures have devised various forms of divination, such as:

AEROMANCY: divination from the sky and air.
ALECTRYOMANCY: divination from a black hen.
ALEUROMANCY: divination by fortune cookies.
ALOMANCY: divination by salt.
APANTOMANCY: divination from chance meetings with animals or birds.
ARITHMANCY: divination through numbers and letter values, an ancient form of numerology.

ASTRAGLOMANCY: divination with dice.

AUGURY: divination by the flight of birds. Also the art, ability or practice of divination in general. See also AUGUR.

AUSTROMANCY: divination by wine.

AXIOMANCY: divination by an ax or hatchet.

BELOMANCY: divination by the tossing or balancing of arrows; one of the most ancient types of divination.

BIBLIOMANCY: divination by books.

BOTANOMANCY: divination by the burning of tree branches and leaves.

CAPNOMANCY: divination through the study of smoke rising up from a fire.

CARTOMANCY: divination with cards.

CATOPTROMANCY: divination using a mirror turned to the moon to catch lunar rays.

CAUSIMOMANCY: divination from objects placed in a fire.

CEPHALOMANCY: divination from the head or skull of a goat.

CARAUNOSCOPY: divination from thunder and lightning.

CEROSCOPY: divination with wax.

CHEIROMANCY: divination through the study of the lines of the palm.

CLEIDOMANCY: divination by dangling a key.

CLEROMANCY: divination using pebbles.

CRITOMANCY: divination from barley cakes.

CROMNIOMANCY: divination from onion sprouts.

CYCLOMANCY: divination by a turning wheel.

DACTYLOMANCY: divination by a dangling ring.

DAPHNOMANCY: divination from the crackling laurel branches in an open fire.

DEMONOMANCY: divination through the aid of demons.

FIRE SCRYING: divination by scrying (or gazing) into the burning embers of a fire.

GEOMANCY: divination from drawings.

HIEROMANCY: divination from objects of ancient sacrifice.

HIPPOMANCY: divination from horses.

HYDROMANCY: divination by water.

ICHTHYOMANCY: divination from fish.

LIBANOMANCY: divination by incense.

LITHOMANCY: divination by the color of stones or beads.

MARGARITOMANCY: divination with pearls.

METAGNOMY: divination while under a hypnotic trance.

METEOROMANCY: divination from meteors and similar phenomena.

MYOMANCY: divination from rats or mice.

NECROMANCY: divination through communication with spirits of the dead.

NUMEROLOGY: divination using numbers.

OCULOMANCY: divination by the reading of eyes.

OINOMANCY: divination from the wind.

ONEIROMANCY: divination by dreams.

ONOMATOMANCY: divination by proper names.

OOMANTIA: divination using eggs.

OPHIOMANCY: divination by serpents.

ORNITHOMANCY: divination by birds.

PEGOMANCY: divination using bubbling fountains of water.

PESSOMANCY: divination through pebbles.

PSYCHOMANCY: divination by men's souls and affections.

PYROMANCY: divination by fire.

RABDOMANCY: divination using a wand or stick.

RHAPSODOMANCY: divination through books of poetry.

ROADOMANCY: divination by the stars.

SAXON WANDS: divination using seven wands made from wood dowels.

SCIOMANCY: divination by shadows.

SCRYING: divination from images seen in a crystal ball or gazing mirror; crystal-gazing; mirror-gazing.

SIDEROMANCY: divination by burning straws on a hot iron.

SORTILEGE: divination by casting lots.

SPODOMANCY: divination from cinders or soot.

TASSEOGRAPHY: divination by reading tea leaves.

TEPHRAMANCY: divination from the ashes of a burned tree trunk.

THEOMANCY: divination by spirits.

THERIOMANCY: divination by beasts.

TUPHRAMANCY: divination by ashes.

TYPOMANCY: divination by coagulation of cheese.

XYLOMANCY: divination from wood.

DIVINING ROD: a forked stick or branch used to find subterranean water or hidden buried treasure by bending downward when held over the source.

DIVINITY: a god or goddess.

DIVINIZE: to regard or worship as a god or goddess.

DJINNI: see JINNI

DOWSE: to use a divining rod.

E

EARTH: one of the four elemental signs.

EARTH SIGNS: the astrological signs attributed to the element of earth are Capricorn, Taurus and Virgo.

ECTOPLASM: a mysterious white substance which emanates from some spiritualist mediums when in a trance.

ELDER: a witch who has graduated to the Third Degree of Witchcraft.

ELEMENTAL SIGNS: the signs of air, earth, fire and water. Air is the symbol of the mind and the reaching beyond of oneself. Earth is the symbol of strength, fertility and the emotions. Fire is the symbol of energy, individuality and identity. Water is the symbol of life and the spirit.

ENOCH: a seer or adept of the Secret Wisdom.

ENOCHIAN MAGICK: a powerful system of magick, similar to the Kabbalah and Yoga.

ESBAT: a regular meeting of a coven that is held during the full moon at least 13 times a year. (For further information, see Chapter II—The Esbat.)

E.S.P.: extrasensory perception.

EVIL EYE: the supernatural power to cause harm, misfortune or death to others by an angry or venomous glance.

EVOCATION: to call out, to bring forth from within to the outside, or to summon up a deity or demon from a position of equality. It is practiced in ceremonies primarily to bring out from within the magickal qualities of the magician.

EXORCISM: the expulsion of an evil spirit or demon from a person by a command, ritual or special prayer.

F

FAMILIAR: an attendant spirit that appears in the form of a cat, lizard, hare, toad or other small animal to aid a witch in the practice of magick.

According to legend, the witch must prick her finger every time the familiar performs a service and feed it a drop of her blood.

FAUSTIAN MAGICK: the evocation of demons.

FETISH: a material object that is believed to possess magickal or supernatural powers.

FIRE: one of the four elemental signs.

FIRE OF AZRAEL: a scrying fire.

FIRE SIGNS: the astrological signs attributed to the element of fire are Aries, Leo and Sagittarius.

FORECAST: a prediction concerning future events; to predict the future.

G

GENETHLIALOGY: the esoteric science, art and practice of calculating the future from the influence of the stars at the time of a person's birth.

GENIE: same as JINNI

GNOMES: elemental spirits of the earth.

GRAPHOLOGY: the analysis of character from handwriting.

GRIMOIRE: a text book of magick.

GRIS-GRIS: a powerful voodoo charm, prepared at the time of a full moon and filled with various offerings to a loa or voodoo spirit.

H

HAGGING: the act of projecting the astral body or "changing the skin" by means of singing a special charm song, according to the magicians of the West Indies.

HANDFASTING: a beautiful Wiccan ceremony that joins a man and a woman "for as long as love shall last" and allows them to freely go their separate ways if they should ever fall out of love with each other. The ceremony is performed during the waxing moon by the priest and priestess of the coven. White robes and flowers are usually worn by all attending, although some covens prefer to work skyclad. Rings of gold or silver with the names of the bride and groom inscribed on them in runes are traditionally exchanged in addition to their love vows.

HANDPARTING: a ceremony that dissolves the Wiccan marriage partnership of a man and a woman.

HATHA YOGA: the practice of physical postures and breathing exercises to attain spiritual integration.

HERMETIC MAGICK: a form of white magick, dating back to the First Century A.D., that combines Egyptian magickal knowledge with other traditions.

HEXAGRAM: a powerful occult symbol made up of two triangles, one superimposed on the other, used to master spirits and banish influences of evil. The two triangles, one pointing up and the other pointing down, are a symbol of man as God. The triangles also symbolize the elements of fire and water. In alchemy, the hexagram stands for distillation and the philosophers' stone, which is said to be composed of fire and water.

HIGH MAGICK: the transformation of the self to the higher self. Some aspects of high magick involve detailed and elaborate spirit-conjuring rites.

HOODOO HANDS: magick charms used to bring the wearer good luck, or to bring illness or death if directed against an enemy.

HORARY ASTROLOGY: an astrological method that uses charts for answering questions and/or solving problems.

HOROSCOPE: an astrological chart of the heavenly bodies that shows the relative positions of the planets at a certain moment in time. Given the exact time and place of birth, an astrologer can cast a person's horoscope from which he or she can define the subject's character and advise future courses of action.

HOROSCOPY: the art and practice of casting astrological horoscopes.

HOUNFOR: a clearing on which peristyle sanctuaries for voodoo loas have been erected.

HOUNGAN: a voodoo priest. The word derives from the Fon language of Dahomey and Togo, meaning literally "the master of a god."

HOUNSIS: a voodoo initiate.

I

I CHING (THE BOOK OF CHANGES): an ancient Chinese science of synchronicity, dating back to the very beginning of Chinese civilization, which is based on a group of 64 six-line drawings called hexagrams that describe the patterns of change and transformation. I Ching (pronounced ee-jing) teaches that the womb of the universe is a limited, imperceptible void—T'ai Chi, the Absolute. In it, everything has its being and each owes its individuality to a particular combination of Yin (negative) and Yang (positive). For I Ching to be consulted for advice or answers to questions, three coins are tossed or a counting game with 50 yarrow sticks is played so that one of the hexagrams, comes up randomly. When properly interpreted, the hexagrams reveal either fortune or misfortune that can be used in divination and for personal consultation.

IDOL: an image or inanimate object representing a divine being. In certain beliefs, the idol is thought to possess power in itself and is often worshipped as though it was the actual god or goddess.

ILLUMINATI: a magickal and kabbalistic sect of occultists also known as "The Enlightened Ones."

IMAGE MAGICK: a form of black magick that uses dolls made of clay, cloth or other material to seduce, harm or kill the person whom the doll is made to represent.

IMP: a witch's familiar.

IMPRECATION: a curse, the act of invoking a curse.

INCANTATION: a ritual recitation of words of power or special phrases in order to produce a magickal effect.

INCUBUS: a demon or evil spirit that takes on the shape of a handsome man and seduces sleeping women in order to possess their souls.

INVOCATION: the act of summoning or conjuring a spirit, demon or deity by incantation.

J

JINNI: according to Moslem legend, a spirit capable of assuming human form and exercising supernatural influence over human beings.

JINX: a person or thing that attracts bad luck or misfortune; to bring bad luck or cause misfortune.

JETTATURA: a person possessed by the power of the evil eye.

JUJU: an object used as an amulet, magickal charm or fetish by the sorcerers of West Africa.

K

KABBALAH: a secret occult theosophy of rabbinical origin
   based on esoteric interpretations of the Hebrew scrip-
   tures. The kabbalah appears as an elaborate system of
   magick, but it is actually a tool for achieving mystic
   union with God. It teaches that there are 72 names of
   God and that the universe is made up of four planes
   of being. (Also spelled cabala, cabbala, kabala and
   qabbalah.)
KARMA: the law of cause-and-effect that applies to all of
   our actions and their consequences in this life or in
   future incarnations.
KELPIES: water spirits often taking the form of a horse.
KUNDALINI YOGA: a branch of yoga that teaches integration
   through the physical and mental control of dormant
   energy in the human body referred to as the
   Kundalini.

L

LEMURES: spirits of the dead.

LEVITATION: the rising into the air and floating of objects or persons by supernatural forces, magick or telekinetic powers.

LIBATION: wine poured on an altar, on the body of a sacrificed animal, on the ground or on a fire as an offering to the Goddess and/or the Horned God.

LITHOBOLIA: poltergeist spirits who bombard dwellings with showers of stones or rocks.

LITHOMANCY: a modern form of divination utilizing the reflections of color from precious stones or beads to draw omens. A blue reflection signifies good luck; black or gray foretells misfortune; red means love and/or marriage; yellow denotes betrayal; green is the sign of success; purple indicates sorrow.

LOAS: voodoo spirits, sometimes called gods.

LYCANTHROPE: a werewolf.

LYCANTHROPY: the magickal or supernatural ability to assume the physical form and characteristics of a wolf.

M

MAGE: a master magician.

MAGICIAN: a nonreligious practitioner of magick; one who summons demons or spirits to work magick but does not worship deities or follow any Wiccan tradition.

MAGICK: the art, science and practice of producing supernatural effects, causing change to occur in conformity and controlling events in nature with will. As a tool of witchcraft, the old spelling of the word with the final "K" is used to distinguish it from the magic of stage conjuring and illusion.

MAGICK SQUARES: a powerful talisman made of rows of numbers or letters of the alphabet arranged in a square.

MALEDICT: to pronounce a curse.

MALEDICTION: a curse.

MAMBO: a voodoo priestess.

MANES: spirits of the dead.

MANTRA: a chant.

MANTRA YOGA: a branch of yoga that uses the chanting of holy words to seek union with the godhead.

MEDIUM: a gifted person through whom the spirits of the dead speak and act.

METOPOSCOPY: the reading of a person's character from the lines of the forehead.

N

NATAL CHART: an astrological map showing the positions of the sun, moon and planets at the exact moment of an individual's birth.

NYMPH: a female water spirit.

O

OBEAH: a form of African-originated sorcery that involves the use of fetishes.

OCCULT: the spiritual sciences.

OCCULTISM: the study of occult powers, supernatural influences and other phenomena beyond the realm of ordinary human comprehension.

OCCULTIST: a person who studies the occult.

ODIC FORCE: an energy phenomenon which emanates from magnets and crystals and is perceived by psychic sensitive persons as a blue (negative) or yellowish-red (positive) glowing light. It can be physically transferred from one substance to another and from one person to another. Odic Force, sometimes called *Od* for short, was discovered by German scientist Baron Karl von Reichenbach (1788–1869), who named it after the Norse god Odin.

OFFERING: a presentation made to the Goddess, Horned God or other deity as an act of religious worship or sacrifice.

THE OLD RELIGION: another name for the practice of witchcraft.

OMEN: any phenomenon or thing that is interpreted as a sign of good luck or misfortune.

ORACLE: a priest or transmitter of prophesies at a shrine consecrated to the worship and consultation of a prophetic deity.

OUIJA: a board with the letters of the alphabet, numbers

and the words "yes" and "no" printed on it. A heart-shaped pointer called a planchette moves around the board to spell out telepathic and spirit-guided messages when touched by the fingertips of one or more persons.

P

PALMISTRY: see CHEIROMANCY

PARAPSYCHOLOGY: the branch of natural science that investigates extrasensory perception, psychokinesis and other psychic phenomena not explainable by known natural laws.

PE: a small stone altar used in voodoo ceremonies.

PENTAGRAM: a protective and magickal five-pointed star that symbolizes the four elements plus the spirit.

PHILOSOPHERS' STONE: a mystical substance manufactured through long and complicated alchemical processes with the power to perfect matter and turn other materials into gold when mixed with them.

PHILTRE: a love potion.

PHRENOLOGY: the psychic science, art and practice of reading the formations of the human head.

PHYSIOGNOMY: a modern psychic science, art and practice of character analysis from the physical appearance of the facial features; face-reading.

PK: psychokinesis.

PLANCHETTE: the triangular pointer from an Ouija board that is used to spell out spirit-guided messages when touched by the fingertips of one or more persons. With a pencil attached, the planchette can also be used for automatic writing.

POPPET: a specially prepared herb-stuffed cloth doll that is used in sympathetic magick love spells and healing rituals to represent the person at whom the spell is directed.

POSSESSION: a phenomenon in which a spirit, good or evil,

takes control of a spiritualist medium in trance. (See also DEMONIC POSSESSION.)

POTION: a magickal tea or brew.

PRACTICAL MAGICK: magick that is concerned with things of the earth, harmony with nature, seasons and cycles, and performed with the aid of simple, common implements.

PRANA: a powerful healing energy which emanates from the human body. It is controlled by the mind, possesses polarity and has properties similar to other forms of energy but is a distinct force unto itself.

PRECOGNITION: extrasensory perception of future events, usually through dreams; psychic awareness of the future.

PREDICTION: a foretelling of the future.

PREMONITION: a psychic sense or intuitive feeling about future events before they happen; presage.

PRESAGE: an intuitive feeling that indicates or warns of a future occurrence; to predict or foretell a future event.

PRESENTMENT: a premonition.

PROPHECY: a prediction made by a prophet.

PROPHESY: to predict the future or to speak as a prophet.

PROPHET: a gifted person who speaks as the interpreter through whom a divinity expresses its will; a soothsayer or predictor; a person who receives symbolic spiritual messages from a god or goddess.

PROPHETESS: a female prophet.

PSI: psychic phenomena.

PSYCHOKINESIS: the production of motion in inanimate objects by the exercise of psychic mind powers.

PSYCHOMETRY: the art and practice of receiving psychic impressions from physical objects.

Q

QUERENT: a person whose fortune is being told by use of tarot cards.

R

RAJA YOGA: a branch of yoga that is devoted to the control of the mind.

REINCARNATION: the rebirthing of the same soul in another physical body. Reincarnation is an ancient belief that is part of many religions, including Wicca.

RETRIBUTION: a reward or punishment given in a future life based on the performance of good or evil in the present lifetime; karma (See THREE- FOLD LAW)

RUNES: letters of a secret magickal alphabet that spell words of power. Runes are written, painted or carved on ritual tools, magician's robes, talismans, amulets, witches' jewelry and other things to charge the object with power. There are three main categories of runes: Anglo-Saxon, Germanic and Scandinavian. Their variations and subdivisions include the Druidic Ogam Bethluisnion, Egyptian hieroglyphics, Theban Script, Pictish, Celestial, Malachim and Passing the River.

S

SABBAT: a joyous witches' festival of merriment and feasting. The witches' sabbat is a time to rejoice, sing,
   dance, chant, honor the God and Goddess, and give
   thanks. Magick is seldom performed during a sabbat
   unless absolutely necessary. Eight sabbats are held
   during the course of a year: Candlemas, Beltane,
   Lammas, Samhain, the Spring Equinox, the Summer
   Solstice, the Autumnal Equinox and the Winter
   Solstice, also known as Yule.
SALAMANDERS: elemental spirits of fire.
SEANCE: a gathering of persons to contact and receive
   messages from the spirits of the dead. Usually it is
   held in the dark or by candlelight at a table where all
   persons attending are seated with hands joined
   together to form a circle. At all seances, at least one
   medium must be present.
SEER: a male clairvoyant.
SEERESS: a female clairvoyant.
SEPHIROT: the 10 emanations of God which are meditated
   upon as the central part of kabbalistic doctrine. The 10
   Sephirot consist of: crown, wisdom, intelligence, love,
   justice, beauty, firmness, splendor, foundation and
   kingdom.
SEX MAGICK: a potent form of magick that uses the sexual
   experience and orgasm to generate the power to work
   magick.
SHAMAN: a priest or person of psychic sensitivity who possesses arcane knowledge and the ability to control the
   spirit forces and communicate with the divine.

SIGNIFICATOR: a certain tarot card that is used to represent the person whose cards are being read.

SKYCLAD: naked, used especially in connection with modern pagan ritual.

SMUDGING: the burning of incense to drive away negative forces and to purify the space in which white magick will be performed.

SOLITARY: a witch, male or female, who practices any form of magick without a coven.

SOOTHSAYER: a clairvoyant.

SORCERER: a male practitioner of sorcery.

SORCERESS: a female practitioner of sorcery.

SORCERY: the use of supernatural power either for material gain or to harm others, often through the support of evil spirits or demons.

SPELL: an incantational formula.

SUCCUBUS: a demon or evil spirit that takes on the shape of a beautiful woman and seduces sleeping men in order to possess their souls; a female incubus.

SYLPHS: elemental spirits of the air.

T

TALISMAN: a manmade object of any shape or material charged with magickal properties to bring good luck, fertility and ward off evil. To formally charge a talisman with power, it must first be inscribed and then consecrated. Inscribing the talisman with a sun sign, moon sign, birthdate, runic name or other magickal symbol personalizes it and gives its purpose.

TAROT: a deck of 78 cards used for reading the past, the future and fortune. The deck is divided into two parts: the Minor Arcana and the Major Arcana. The Minor Arcana consists of 56 divinatory cards divided into four suits of 14 cards each: swords, pentacles, wands and cups. The Major Arcana consists of 22 highly symbolic trump cards with colorful allegorical figures. The various methods of tarot card-reading include the Celtic Cross method, the Golden Dawn method (modified by Aleister Crowley), and the Oracles of Julia Orsini, an ancient French method that uses a significator card plus 42 other cards.

TELEPATHY: the transfer of thoughts from one mind into another.

THIRD EYE: the human body's highest source of power, supernormal sight and clairvoyant vision. The Third Eye is invisible and located in the middle of the forehead.

THREE-FOLD LAW: the Wiccan belief that if a witch does good, he or she will get it back threefold in the same lifetime. Whatever harm a witch does to others is also returned threefold.

THURIBLE: an incense vessel (or censer) used in magickal ceremonies.

TRANCE: a state in which a medium loses consciousness, thus permitting spirits to enter and speak or act through the medium's physical body.

TREE OF LIFE: a kabbalistic diagram showing the 10 Sephirot (emanations of God) and their relationship to each other.

TRUE MAGICK: white magick, magick that is performed for good purposes, to heal or to help others.

U

UNDINES: elemental spirits of water.

V

VAMPIRISM: the practice of drinking human blood. In folklore, a vampire is the reanimated corpse of a dead person that rises from its grave at night and sucks the blood from the throats of living humans or animals.

VEVES: intricate symbolic voodoo emblems that are drawn on the ground with flour or ashes to invoke the various loas, or voodoo spirits, which they represent.

VOODOO: a primitive system of magick, brought to Haiti and the Caribbean by African slaves. It involves the use of both black and white magick and is characterized by fetish worship, animal sacrifices, frenzied drum dances and zombies.

VOODOOISM: the practice of voodoo as well as the view of life and death embodied in the voodoo cult.

W

WARLOCK; a word stemming from the Old English WAER-LOGA meaning an "oath breaker" and used derogatorily by the Church as a name for a male witch. In Wicca, the word Warlock is seldom, if ever, used. Both male and female practitioners of the Craft are called witches.

WATER: one of the four elemental signs.

WATER SIGNS: the astrological signs attributed to the element of water are Cancer, Pisces and Scorpio.

WEREWOLF: a man transformed into a wolf through supernatural power or black magick; a lycanthrope.

WHITE MAGICK: positive magick that is practiced for good purposes or as a counter to evil.

WICCA: a monistic and pantheistic religion created in the mid-20th century in the United Kingdom by an English witch named Gerald Gardner.

WICCAN: an adherent of the neo-pagan religion known as Wicca.

WICCANING: a Wiccan birth rite by which a baby is given a name by its parents, anointed on the forehead with salted water by the coven priestess, and then passed through the smoke of incense by its mother as a gesture of purification.

WICCAN REDE: a simple and benevolent moral code of Wicca that is as follows: "An it harm none, do what thou wilt."

WIDDERSHINS: an old Scottish word meaning "counterclockwise."

WITCH: a person, male or female, who practices the ancient art and science of magick; a follower of the

Old Religion; a Wiccan. According to the American Heritage Dictionary of the English Language, the word WITCH stems from the Old English "WICCE" (feminine) meaning a witch, and "WICCA" (masculine) meaning a wizard. Many modern witches and writers of the occult argue however that the word WICCA is Anglo-Saxon meaning "the wise one" or "a magician who weakens the power of evil."

WITCHCRAFT: the art and practices of a witch. Also known as The Old Religion or The Craft, witchcraft dates to pre-Christian times and utilizes magickal or supernatural powers to influence people or events. The concept of witchcraft and the belief in its existence have existed in divergent cultures around the world throughout recorded history. Witchcraft can be secular (incorporating the worship of pagan deities, for example) or non-secular.

WITCHES' LADDER: a special string with nine knots used by black magick witches as a powerful magickal weapon to harm or kill enemies.

WITCHES' SABBAT: see SABBAT

WIZARD: a male magician or witch. The word WIZARD derives from the Middle English WIS, meaning "wise."

WIZARDRY: the art, skill or practice of a magician.

X

xylomancy: the occult science, art and practice of drawing omens from pieces of wood by interpreting their shapes and formations or by the way they burn when placed upon a fire.

Y

YA SANG: a form of black magick, performed mainly in the northeastern part of Thailand, which incorporates poisonous plants to bring about abdominal disorders, intoxications, and sometimes even death.

Z

ZAZEN: a form of Zen meditation.

ZOBOP: a group of voodoo sorcerers who band together for power.

ZODIAC: a circular band in the sky through which the planets are seen to move. It is divided into 12 equal sections called zodiac signs, each 30 degrees wide, bearing the name of a constellation for which it was originally named but with which it no longer coincides due to the precession of the vernal and autumnal equinoxes. The 12 signs of the zodiac are Aries the ram, Taurus the bull, Gemini the twins, Cancer the crab, Leo the lion, Virgo the virgin, Libra the balance, Scorpio the scorpion, Sagittarius the archer, Capricorn the goat, Aquarius the water-bearer and Pisces the fish.

THE ZOHAR: the Bible of Mysticism. First published in the 13th century, it is believed to be the composition of Rabbi Simon ben Yochai, a 2nd century Jewish luminary renowned as a great mystic. The Zohar deals with nearly every aspect and theme of the occult, and its teachings have exerted a great influence on the kabbalah as well as the world of the occult.

ZOMBIE: a "living" corpse without mind, feeling or will of its own, reanimated by the occult power of a voodoo sorcerer-priest and used mainly as a slave.

Index

Connect with Us

Visit us online at
KensingtonBooks.com
to read more from your favorite authors, see books
by series, view reading group guides, and more.